# EXTREME

# OUTDOOR ADVENTURES

# EXTREME

## OUTDOOR ADVENTURES

### WHO SURVIVES AND WHY

Larry Mueller and

Marguerite Reiss

THE LYONS PRESS
Guilford, Connecticut
An imprint of The Globe Pequot Press

The Lyons Press is an imprint of The Globe Pequot Press.

10   9   8   7   6   5   4   3   2   1

Printed in the United States of America
Designed by Diane Gleba Hall

ISBN 978-1-59921-200-5

Library of Congress Cataloging-in-Publication Data is available on file.

To survivors Peter Reiss and Jim Reiss. And to: Drs. Mark Mills, Bruce Klunzinger, Jennifer Gilmore; John Reiss; Attys. Clinton Canady and Eric Williams; Will Reiss, Kerry Fitzpatrick, Gail Brown, Mike Reiss, Dick Schneider, Sharon Azar, Marion Heider, Melinda Milheim, and David Reiss.

—MARGUERITE REISS

And—

To all the survivors of extreme outdoor adventures, and to their courageous friends and family members who have helped save them.

To my great-grandchildren and beyond, born and unborn, I dedicate this book and offer my hope that participation in the natural world will develop your survival skills and otherwise enrich your lives.

—LARRY MUELLER

CONTENTS

## THE WHYS, HOWS, AND MAYBES OF SURVIVAL

DR. BILL WENNEN, a Fairbanks, Alaska, plastic surgeon who has done reconstruction work on numerous bear attack victims, sees a definite thread that connects people who survive extreme emergencies. "It's attitude," he told me. "It's 90 percent attitude and 10 percent preparation. Those who don't have enough will give up and die."

Survivors don't even think about giving up, Wennen says. They keep trying to find a way out of their situation until they discover what works.

That's very similar to what Portland, Oregon, psychologist Dr. Al Siebert found in his study of survivors, which led to his book *The Survivor Personality*. Dr. Siebert found that survivors are those individuals who aren't locked into single ways of doing things, and aren't dependent on familiar support systems. When one thing isn't working, they try something else.

Survivors got that way by challenging themselves, seeing what they could get away with as they grew up and beyond. That required tolerant parents who were willing to put up with some cuts and bruises, and were able to pass along some sound advice, rooted in common sense. Good parents should be taking their children on safe adventures when they're small. The outdoors is the perfect place for them. Adventures and challenges enlarge as the youngsters grow.

I was too busy in the outdoors to have time to join the Boy Scouts. Football, however, provided me a foundation lesson that always comes to mind when I read about traits of smart survivors.

In one particular high school football game, I was on the defensive line to the right of center. Two plays in a row, two opposite linemen were able to double-team and overpower me, as one dove behind me and the other pushed me over the first guy. As we lined up for a third play, I heard one whisper to the other, "It works on this guy every time."

That woke me up. When the play started, the same fellow dove behind me as I dodged away from him to my right. The guy in front lunged over to meet me, but I instantly dodged to my left and raced through an opening in the line to tackle the fullback. The life lesson I took away from that was, don't do the same dumb thing twice, or have the same dumb reaction more than once, a match for some of Dr. Siebert's findings.

In his continued studies of survivors, Dr. Siebert found them to be more resilient than other people in general. He says they handle life's setbacks better. They are optimistic, self-confident, psychologically complex, use creative problem solving, handle pressure with humor, and are less likely to experience frequent anger. Older survivors become accustomed to things working out well. Many don't retire from their careers because they enjoy the benefits of doing important work.

Seibert also notes that resiliency can be developed and increased at any age, but can't be taught by standard training methods. Resilient people can only be coached into developing inborn abilities through self-managed learning. Challenging their own individuality works best.

Another interest of Dr. Siebert's is intuition. He says he developed his by listening to it. One morning he awoke at 4 A.M. with a strong urge to go to the beach, and was already at the door when a hunch told him to take his knife and gloves along. When he arrived, he turned north and felt he was walking in the wrong direction. Turning back south, it seemed right. At that point, he felt he was being led to something, and studied the shore debris until he saw movement. It was a "dark bird with an orange beak" entangled in monofilament fishing line with bobber and hook still attached. He touched the bird, then gently put his left hand around its neck. The bird relaxed. It took about five minutes to carefully cut it free. Another morning, he had an urge to carry a book of matches with him to the river, for no reason he could think of. Walking along the shore, he noticed a rather unkempt man coming toward him. As he got close, the fellow asked, "Do you have any matches?" Not at all surprised, Siebert produced the matches from his pocket and handed them to the fellow without even breaking stride.

Clearly, as Captain Thorne Tasker, whom you'll meet in Chapter 12 of this book, said, "The mind is a powerful thing. People underestimate it." It took superhuman strength to do what he did as the crabbing vessel *Nowitna* was sinking in the Bering Sea—strength like those average, normal people who single-handedly lift cars off their injured loved ones. Although he wasn't aware of it until the emergency had ended, Tasker understands that he was accessing a mental power, not just a physical one.

After it was all over, and Tasker had rented a car, he reached out with his left hand—the same hand that gripped the down sloping steel cable so tightly that the rolling vessel couldn't pitch him off into the sea—and tried to push the button with his thumb to open the door. He couldn't. It was then that he remembered breaking that thumb a couple days earlier. Never once through that entire emergency at sea had his thumb ever hurt.

Dr. Wennen says we know little for sure about how the brain could have doused the pain and caused superhuman power in that boat captain's hand, but we do know that superhuman power probably couldn't materialize in a body or limb that's in pain on account of what it's doing. He does, however, offer an explanation about how we seem to automatically "know" what to do in an emergency. That could come from an accumulated lifetime of experiences stored deep inside the brain. Those experiences are not normally accessible, but they're released in an instant when we're threatened by an extreme emergency. Also, some of the memories deep in the brain could be, in part, a result of the history of the species. The animal species have the same phenomenon, and we call it instinct.

But could instinct be inheritable? A Russian study of DNA, in which linguists as well as geneticists were involved, found language patterns in the 95 percent of DNA that most geneticists think is useless and call junk DNA. The study generated speculation that this 95 percent could be a huge storage and communications area, making possible a stored species history or instinct. It would also make possible intuition, a mom's "knowing" that her children are in trouble, twins in different places "knowing" what the other is going through, remote healing by prayer, and, yes, people in extreme emergencies "knowing" what to do. It could even house the trigger mechanism that shuts down pain, allowing seemingly super strength.

As *Outdoor Life* magazine's Hunting Dogs editor for twenty-four years, I always had a great interest in instinctual behavior. And as *Reader's Digest*'s Alaska reporter for twenty years, I did also. The pointing instinct, for example, was developed over the past 200 years, and based in wild canines' already-present instinct to sniff out prey, stalk closer, and hesitate long enough to zero in on the prey's exact location before leaping to catch it.

By patient training, we made dogs stop wherever they were when they first sniffed the prey, and to stand there in hesitation until we flushed the birds. By selectively breeding those that train most easily, today we have dogs that instinctively point the first bird they ever smell. Is instinct, then, a collection of inherited memories?

In just his own lifetime, my Virginia turkey-hunting buddy John Byrne did for his dogs what took 200 years in pointers. He had an English setter–pointer–Plott hound cross named Junior that he considered the perfect turkey dog. An Angus cattle breeder, John is very savvy in breeding techniques, and he inbred Junior until warning signs cropped up. Then he backed off and made an outcross to start a second line. Junior was sound stock, and his pups made it to 15/16 Junior without problems. That's not 100 percent Junior and never could be, even if carried to 31/32 and beyond. Math and logic suggest that since the pups are never 100 percent Junior, they can never be Junior's equal. The opposite was true. Over the generations, John noticed that these pups were becoming easier to train than Junior ever was. The 15/16 pups were "naturals" requiring little training beyond taking them hunting. To my mind, there is no way this could happen without an accumulation of inherited memory.

Professor Marion Diamond at the University of California was one step from having the answer. Working with rats, she found that those that were mentally challenged actually developed thicker cortexes. And that does prove how challenging ourselves makes better survivors. Some of Dr. Diamond's rats were fed and watered in plain boxes. The others had toys to deal with and learn from. These learned quicker how to get through a maze. They could also be placed in a tank of water with a somewhat submerged rock or mound and be expected to quickly find that resting place when they tired of swimming—and remember where it is. The unchallenged rats could not.

Other universities have studied the greater cortex growth of challenged rats, but I have not found a study that focused on inherited cortex growth. In the interest of encouraging the development of greater numbers of humans with survival personalities, this is basic science that still needs to be done.

We may never learn everything about the mind, but one thing is certain: the mind is our most powerful tool in survival. Use it. Challenge it. Be ready to improvise, adapt, and overcome.

—LARRY MUELLER

## THE SPIRIT OF SURVIVAL

Faced with a life-threatening situation and obviously terrible odds, basic human reasoning might say, "End of the road." But survivors of these harrowing situations show that there's something in us all that can greatly surpass empirical reasoning.

Despite unyielding pain and horror, there springs up from seemingly broken and overwhelmed people a drive to take charge of one's immediate destiny. I have heard the tone of this drive in the voice of a woman cleaved by an airplane propeller, far away in the Alaskan bush. I saw its glint in the eyes of two hunters disfigured by flames but who willed themselves to live. I have felt it myself when a rapist gripped my throat and I couldn't scream. Indeed, my own experience has driven me to ask the question of many survivors I have interviewed: "What kept you alive?"

"Guts," responded a seventy-year-old torn up by a grizzly. "I had no choice," a dying man said of his cancer. A woman who packed herself in ice to keep from losing her unborn child put her situation "in God's hands," she said, but she's the one who made the first move. She delivered a healthy baby. An Air Force para-jumper, without a wetsuit and strapped to an injured seaman in a Stokes Litter on a fishing trawler, said, "I denied myself looking down and made myself look only where I was going, upward and outward, never looking where I had been," as high seas swept the boat out from under him and he swung from the rescue cable attached to the helicopter above.

When the six-foot-four rapist stepped into my kitchen right behind me, and turned to lock the back door he had just come through, an inner voice said, *Crouch down and shove one foot out the screen door to the ground.* I kicked the door open, and my foot hooked a trellis, and I dragged down a bird feeder, and several flowerpots and vines. The sudden crash of all that stuff gave me the fleeting moment I needed to struggle past my attacker and get outside where he threw me over three garbage cans, causing even more flowerpots to come raining down in a great dramatic commotion like something out of a movie. "Good timing," a detective later opined about my unthinking decision to throw a foot to the door. "In a case like that you are fighting for seconds."

At some point in our lives each of us faces devastation, a great deficit, or near-total defeat; not just a simple gash across our lives, but something approaching an amputation. We learn once again what we already know from far back in our evolution: that we have undreamed-of powers for demonstrating our coping skills when life turns drastic.

There is a captivating enigma that distinguishes those who can cope from the casualties. The swiftness, grit, clarity of mind, and imperviousness of such people seem beyond a day-to-day reality. And yet, day after day, people prove the human mettle.

This book is addressed to you if you might feel wounded by failure or stress, or feel that one day you could be, for whatever reason, standing in the way of a terrible blow. You can be armed with coping techniques that triumph, and by your sheer survival offer great encouragement to others who struggle themselves.

—MARGUERITE REISS

# 1

*Survivors enjoy taking risks to discover how they'll handle it. It seems paradoxical, but risk-takers survive much better than those whose main concerns are safety and security.*

IMAGINE you're dropped without warning into a wilderness disaster. You could be lost, injured, caught in a storm, threatened with hypothermia, or whatever your worst nightmare might be. Think quickly: What's the key to your survival? Is it gear and things you might need? Perhaps layered clothes, a tube tent, waterproof fire starting materials, extra food, a compass, water-purification tablets, or a first-aid kit? Or is it skill and technique? Perhaps knowing how to build windbreaks, shelters, and fires, staying put to be rescued, going hungry if finding food costs more calories than it provides?

The lists go on and on. You find them in every article and manual on the subject. They're valid and valuable. Heed their advice. But the lists don't provide the real key to survival. That element comes from within. And nowhere is it more evident than among people who make their homes in the Arctic.

Randy Crosby, head of the North Slope Borough Search and Rescue Center in Barrow, Alaska, hints at the key to Arctic survival when he says, "Hunters up here don't even entertain the thought of not surviving in our worst weather."

Ben Ahmaogak, fifty-two, was alone on his snowmachine hunting caribou and ice-fishing for grayling and whitefish. Though he had started with a full tank for a planned ten-day trip, he ran into a white-out, became disoriented, and ran out of gas. He was two days overdue when his wife, Florence, called Crosby.

"You have to understand," Crosby responded, "here in the North Slope Borough we have 92,000 square miles, an area the size of Minnesota, and four planes and pilots to cover it."

Although the odds were slim, Crosby piloted a King Air twin-engine turbo prop to look for Ahmaogak. After three days of searching, he got a break. The plane was flying at 500 feet a quarter mile from the Utukok River in the foothills of the Brooks Range when one of the spotters on board thought he saw something. When Crosby's plane circled, Ahmaogak flopped on his back to make himself more visible, kicking his feet for attention.

Ahmaogak had made no fire; for heat he had used a Coleman stove. He was dressed in a lamb-lined parka and had pitched his 7-by-9-foot white canvas wall tent against a bluff for a windbreak. For additional windbreak, he had excavated snow and set the tent 3 feet below the surface level, an Eskimo trick. The tent stakes couldn't be driven into the frozen ground, so he had gathered willows, bundling and burying them in packed snow to hold the tent ropes.

"By the time we found him," Crosby said, "Ben had been out there in zero to minus-10-degree weather for two weeks. How badly was he shaken by the experience? He simply told us, 'Go get me some gas, and I'll drive home.'"

"I never doubted that I'd make it," is a frequent comment from survivors. Those who endure being stranded in the cold believe that their survival is up to them. Help may come, but they know they have to do their part, as Ahmaogak did.

"The will to live can keep a person going longer than almost anything else," says Lieutenant Colonel Gene Ramsey, former commander of the

210th Air Rescue Squadron at Anchorage. Knowing this, professional rescuers in the North have learned to nourish that will in lost people. Doing so often means flying in forbidding weather at great personal risk. But they know that just the sight of a plane dropping flares is enough to restore hope and confidence, which will likely keep a lost person going. Rescuers can then parachute in later, when safer weather conditions allow.

Experience convinced Colonel Eric Wheaten, former commander of the 71st Air Rescue and Recovery Squadron at Elmendorf Air Force Base in Alaska, that personality influences an individual's will to live. Wheaten was assigned to take nine para-rescuemen on a three-day training exercise. They would be staged only 30 miles from Anchorage, but across an inlet in an isolated area. Temperatures would fall to minus 20 degrees at night.

A flight surgeon, a quite capable doctor, decided to go along and see how his men performed in the field under survival conditions. Wheaten, the doctor, and two para-rescuemen were flown out first by helicopter, along with tents, a chain saw, gas, and food. The remaining gear would follow in the next chopper load. The seven other para-rescuemen would be dropped later.

By late morning, Wheaten realized that the other men and supplies weren't coming. He couldn't know it, but equipment malfunctions had kept all of the other choppers grounded at Elmendorf. The sun was due to set at 2:30 in the afternoon, so Wheaten and the men cut wood, built a fire, and set up two tents over pine boughs to make softer, warmer beds.

The flight surgeon was not helpful. He became cold almost immediately. His morale plummeted. He was clearly despondent. The men slept. Wheaten remained awake to keep an eye on the flight surgeon, who couldn't sleep. That night the doctor bumped the ends of his fingers while adding wood to the fire. In the morning he mistook the blood under his nails for frostbite. This normally excellent doctor had become so distressed that he couldn't make a simple medical diagnosis.

"The problem was that the flight surgeon was heavily dependent upon a game plan, and that plan changed," Wheaten says. "The rest of us kept the fire going, cooked in the little tin cups, and tried to keep his spirits up during a second night. Only on the third morning, when the HC-130 flew over and dropped an emergency kit, did he believe he would be rescued. There was never a real emergency, except in the flight surgeon's mind. But because of his mental attitude, I'm convinced that by himself he would not have lasted twenty-four hours."

In contrast, Thomas Ruland, a fifty-nine-year-old Eskimo, was much less materially prepared when he was lost on a hunting expedition. Though hunting in fur mitts, down pants, snowmachine boots, and a homemade lambskin-lined parka with wolf ruff, he had no tent. He had a thermos with coffee and enough dried caribou for one day. Beyond that, he had only a caribou hide to ward off the elements when he was reported to be several days overdue on the North Slope of the Brooks Range.

Rescuer Gilbert Lincoln remembers that the call came in at 10 P.M., and two snowmachines were dispatched from the Anaktuvuk Pass Rescue Center within the hour. Two more rescuers followed that night. Tracks were found but lost again in the darkness and blowing snow. Finally, in 50-mile-per-hour winds and minus-40-degree temperatures, the rescuers were forced to pitch a tent for shelter. Requests to Barrow for a spotter plane the next morning were denied because of wind conditions.

Despite continuing severe weather the next day, the search up the Anaknivuk Valley resumed. That afternoon, one team discovered an abandoned snowmachine. "They looked around," Lincoln says, "and suddenly, 100 yards away, a person appeared right out of a snowdrift!"

Ruland had dug a small cave in the snow, placed his caribou hide on the ground, and curled up, protected from the bitter wind and cold. When snowmachine trouble had upset his game plan, he adapted without undue fear.

◆

Part of the contrast in these stories lies in the fact that the flight surgeon had been camping just once in his life, and that was in Texas. Ruland was better trained to switch game plans. Traditional Eskimos teach survival skills to their children.

Wheaten suggests that the ability to survive in extreme conditions requires more than conditioning. It also requires the mental ability to ignore reality. "I met a crusty old retired sergeant on the Yukon River who was prospecting for gold in the middle of the winter in minus-40 temperatures," Wheaten says. "He lived in a cabin not much bigger than a large desk. He was ignoring reality in order to pursue his fascination for gold."

The inner key to survival seems elusive. The "will to live" is a necessity. But do those three words have a specific meaning? Can we explain what gives one individual more will to live than another?

How about training? Knowing two ways to build a shelter gives you twice the options. Competence inspires confidence. Yet the competent doctor lost his most basic medical capability. That happens to many people threatened by disaster. Is the ability to "ignore reality" the real key?

It's real, all right. But this ability only buys time.

The main factor that seems basic to every survivor is the ability to switch game plans. Indeed, according to Portland, Oregon, psychologist Dr. Al Siebert, "Survivors are those who can give up being one way or the other."

Siebert has been studying survivors since 1953, when he interrupted college to join the Army paratroopers. There, a strong personal interest in survival became wedded to opportunity. Siebert's trainers at Fort Campbell, Kentucky, were from a unit that had been trapped at Inchon, Korea. Only one man in ten had lived through the experience. Siebert wanted to know the reason why.

In studying survivors, Siebert first hypothesized that the best survivalist is the stereotypical male who fits the image, perhaps the stand-up hero who resolutely sticks with his beliefs, commitments, or guns to the bitter end. However, he found little in common among the survivors other than that each man who lived through the Inchon ordeal believed that his survival depended entirely on himself. Beyond that, the soldiers' characteristics were full of puzzling contradictions.

Eventually, Siebert unraveled the puzzle and wrote *The Survivor Personality.* In the book, which studies the psychology of survival, he explains that people with complex personalities were best prepared to survive in extreme conditions. The best survivors are not overly attached to objects, procedures, or beliefs. People who continue to need a plan to follow in life after they mature are not the best survivors, whether in daily affairs or wilderness disasters. The best way to develop a survivor personality, according to Siebert, is to challenge yourself. Survivors enjoy taking risks to discover how they'll handle them, accepting mistakes as learning experiences. Though it seems paradoxical, risk-takers survive much better than those whose main concerns are safety and security.

What some survivors' minds can accomplish for them under extreme circumstances borders on miracle. In fact, when Dr. Janet Shackles, director of Maniilag Medical Center in Kotzebue, Alaska, heard what happened to Morris Sage, she said, "He cannot be alive." Dr. Susan Klingler, who treated Sage, assured her that he was.

Sage, forty-eight, and his close friend, Sayers Tuzroyluk, forty-six, had been hunting caribou on snowmachines for ten hours. Both eat traditional Eskimo foods on a daily basis—seal oil, whale blubber, caribou, polar bear, and so on. At about 8 P.M., with Sage in the lead by 80 yards, the two men were driving their machines on the ice along the edge of a lagoon. In the headlight, Sage saw gravel blown on the ice by the wind, so he turned his machine farther away from shore to avoid the rough grit under his runners. Twenty yards out, the ice shattered, and his machine dove toward bottom, pulling his homemade, flat-bottomed sled behind. Sage let go, losing his mittens, but he stayed on the surface, helped by the buoyancy of his lamb-lined parka.

Tuzroyluk saw a flash of Sage's headlight reflecting in the splash and slowed his machine. The ice was thicker where he was, just 10 feet from shore, but not strong enough to bear heavy weight for very long. Tuzroyluk heard the ice splitting and felt his machine dive out from under him. He swam desperately to reach shore before his heavy clothes became waterlogged. Soaked to the skin, he climbed out with nothing left but his wet clothes. The drop-off, even that close to shore, was so deep that his 10-foot sled vanished with the machine. It carried the extra clothes, long ropes with treble hooks for retrieving seals, and everything else that may have been useful for survival.

The rear end of Sage's sled bobbed back up. Apparently, the large amount of wood in the flat-sled structure, plus perhaps a mostly empty gas tank, had raised the snowmachine off the bottom. Sage grabbed the sled with one hand and struggled to keep it from twisting and turning while pulling his rifle sling off over his head with the other hand.

Freed of the rifle's weight, Sage tried to swim to shore. Not a strong swimmer, he got only a few feet when he realized that his heavy clothes were completely saturated. He felt as if he weighed 600 pounds. Doubting that he could stay afloat, he returned to the sled. With the lights of both machines gone, Tuzroyluk couldn't see Sage, but knew he was in the water and feared he went down with the snowmachine. He started to panic, running up and down the shore crying out in anguish for his friend.

"Hey, bro', don't cry for me yet," Sage called. "I'm still alive!" Relieved, Tuzroyluk looked for something that might help reach Sage. His sled didn't surface, so there was no rope. Tuzroyluk did find a 12-foot limb, though, and began wading out to Sage using the limb to sound the depth. Five feet from shore, Tuzroyluk was up to his waist, and the long stick poking ahead of him failed to touch bottom. There was no way he could survive the swim.

"Morris! I can't get far enough out to reach you!"

Sage asked the Lord to forgive his sins, then called back. "You'll have to go for help," and after a pause added, "Tell my children I loved them." Sage felt weak when he said those words. Tuzroyluk left at a run, but Point Hope was at least five miles away. Sage had faith in Tuzroyluk, but it would take hours. Meanwhile, he could die. As quickly as that thought entered his mind, however, he dismissed it. He remembered an old man telling a story of being on sea ice in January when it broke away from shore. Faced with drifting out to sea or swimming back to shore, the man had dived in.

"Water is not cold," the old man had said, "unless you think it's cold."

Sage wedged his hands between underwater cross-members and rested his chin on the back end of the sled. He began to think about bears hibernating. Even though he did not feel cold, Sage knew his body temperature would fall. But it falls for hibernating bears too, he thought. Their body functions slow down, and they come near death, but they survive. Sage visualized himself as a bear entering hibernation. He would survive.

Sage felt the wind pick up. The water was 28 degrees, 4 degrees below freezing, yet not frozen to the bottom because of salt content. The air temperature had fallen near zero. The wind rose to 20 knots. Sage shook briefly, probably in the first stage of hypothermia as the body temperature falls to 90 degrees. But refusing to believe that the water was cold, he found it didn't feel cold to him. Sage was a bear going into hibernation. He fell asleep, with his chin still on the sled, so that he wouldn't drown.

Tuzroyluk ran as fast as he could, as long as he could. But he was tiring. And he was freezing. Tuzroyluk had experienced hypothermia before. That time he had given up, and if someone had not found him, he would have died.

Halfway to Point Hope, Tuzroyluk's legs began to cramp. Muscles become rigid when body temperatures hit between 90 and 86 degrees. The next step is stupor. But he wouldn't allow that to happen. He was carrying Sage's words: "Tell my children . . ." And Tuzroyluk kept thinking of his own eight youngsters. Tuzroyluk's stiff-legged steps grew shorter. By the time he reached Point Hope, he was staggering to stay on his feet. A truck driver passed him by, probably thinking that Tuzroyluk was drunk. Finally, a man on a three-wheeler stopped and took Tuzroyluk to his brother-in-law, who immediately activated the search-and-rescue unit. Tuzroyluk couldn't go along. He was immobile for another hour.

Twice, Sage remembers waking up, taking a sip of water, and falling back asleep. It surprised him that the water didn't taste saltier. He had watched the ocean overflowing into the lagoon all summer. He hallucinated, seeing Tuzroyluk and Tuzroyluk's wife, Dianne, on the shore.

When the rescuers spotted Sage in the headlights of their truck, he was frozen in, but still talking, though incoherently. They had to chop him out and cut off his frozen parka. Ten more volunteers came out on snowmachines. However, there was little to do but get Sage back to Point Hope, where a plane from the rescue center at Barrow would fly him to the hospital at Kotzebue.

The bear survived his hibernation. But as Dr. Schackles said, survival in 28-degree water lasts 15 or 20 minutes, 30 at most. Sage was in the water more than three hours. How?

"Maybe it's all in your head," Sage says.

Dr. Siebert points out that our scientifically based culture, with its unwillingness to believe anything it cannot immediately prove, may inhibit a person's mental capacity for survival. Native people find it easier to "become" (perhaps through self-hypnosis) another thing (an eagle, bear, and so on) and to think how it would think.

"Our society reduces everything to numbers," Siebert says, "so we lose that ability to imagine very early in school."

Sage thanks God, Tuzroyluk, the rescuers, and the medical people at Kotzebue, but his complete faith kept him alive until others could do their work. Certainly, the survivor, whether in the wilderness or otherwise, requires faith—if not Sage's incredible 100 percent, at least conviction and self-confidence. The will to live is weakened when that confidence is shaken. A strong reason to live can help. So can an outside signal indicating that rescue is eminent. But the greatest strength exists, or fails to exist, in the complexity and flexibility of the personality. Survivors are able to recognize other options and adjust.

## ARE YOU A SURVIVOR?

In his book *The Survivor Personality,* Dr. Al Seibert offers a quick test to identify survivors. Choosing from Columns A and B, select the traits that best describe your personality:

| Column A | Column B |
| --- | --- |
| strong-willed | easygoing |
| gentle | strong |
| serious | humorous |
| calm | emotional |
| involved | detached |
| impulsive | thorough |
| stable | unpredictable |
| trusting | cautious |
| childlike | mature |
| sensible | irrational |
| individualistic | conforming |
| self-confident | self-critical |
| lazy | hardworking |
| shy | bold |

Did you most often find yourself on both sides of the aisle? If so, that's good! No single or multiple personality traits are critical to survival. People with traits in both columns are complex and flexible. They adjust more easily to changing circumstances, which gives them a good chance at surviving in the wilderness.

Most survivors got that trait by challenging themselves since child-hood—seeing what they can get away with. Knees are skinned, toes are stubbed, and sometimes bones are broken, but the setbacks are accepted as lessons in where and when to be more careful. A boy hid a cut finger from view so his new knife would not be confiscated. A young man, who did not believe that fast, roiling floodwaters had undertows that could pull down a strong swimmer, challenged 40 yards of bank-full creek. He swam high in the water, did not fight the current, came out 50 yards downstream, walked 100 yards upstream, then swam back to the start-ing point without ever feeling a tug. More confident than ever in water, he joined the Navy and went to sea.

It's never too late to challenge your abilities and improve your sur-vival skills. Afraid of snakes? Kill one and skin it. The fear is gone, and someday, in a survival situation, you'll be able to kill another, and skin, roast, and eat it to stave off hunger. Just make your confidence-building challenges small, only gradually enlarging them to avoid a surprise disaster.

# 2

*There was no time to think. Chris Brown just knew what he had to do—fight off, with his bare hands, the lion that was attacking his stepson, David Vaught.*

IT HAS LONG been an article of faith that healthy mountain lions never attack human beings. Yet here's a case in which a healthy two-year-old cougar did its best to kill an eight-year-old boy. Thanks to the skill and the determination of a hunter and his hounds that cougar will never try to kill again.

Kim Brown was crying. She had stepped on a column of army ants and one ant had crawled up inside her pants leg, biting as it climbed. Her sobbing in response to the stinging pain and the frustration of being unable to remove the ant quickly could have sounded like an animal in distress to the mountain lion. For whatever reason, the cougar chose to lie and wait just beyond a sharp bend in the trail where anything coming around would be too close to escape.

Chris Brown, Kim's husband, really hadn't wanted to go hiking. The family had just arrived in Big Bend National Park and he wanted to unpack. But David Vaught, his eight-year-old stepson of less than a year, was excited and anxious to look around. The mountainous area differed greatly from the country around Garland, near Dallas, where the family lived. The date was August 2, 1984, and the family was following a circular trail that began and ended at the park's headquarters.

Rattlesnakes are always a possibility in the rocky Southwest, so Chris led off. Every now and again David yelled "snake!" to test his mother's fright reactions. It worked the first few times, but then Kim encountered the army ants. Chris stopped to help her. David and his four-year-old brother Justin walked on. In fact, Justin got ahead of David, but David figured that he was next-in-command and had to watch out for snakes, so he pushed Justin behind him shortly before he turned the bend where the trail darkened as it entered a thicket.

"Mountain lion!" David yelled. He stared in disbelief, transfixed for an instant by the sight of the twitching tail and the laid-back ears.

Nobody believed David's yell. Cougars are shy, secretive creatures and are rarely seen, even from a distance. Besides, David had repeatedly yelled "snakes!" when there were none. But Chris glanced up and felt an instinctive foreboding.

The next thing Chris saw was David three steps into a run with the lion right behind him. David looked back over his left shoulder and the cat leaped, its mouth open almost 180 degrees, like a striking snake's. The cougar dug its hind claws into David's thigh and its front claws deep in both shoulders as its jaws clamped on the boy's head. Just as quickly, the lion relaxed its grip on all but the head. The claws tore out as the lion's weight and momentum carried it over David's body, in an action intended to break the boy's neck. David and the cat fell.

The boy lay limp. His mother screamed in terror, thinking that her son was dead. The snarling mountain lion chewed on David's head. Chris Brown ran at the cat, yelling, trying to frighten it off. The cougar glanced up defiantly, snarled, and then continued its attempt to sink its fangs into David's skull. Running at the lion, Chris kicked at it, and slipped on the slope. He fell alongside the cat and grabbed at it.

Chris could not get hold of the tight skin over the lion's bulging muscles, though his efforts did make the animal pause a moment and turn to look. When the cat turned back to David, Chris grabbed its neck with both hands and pulled.

The lion screamed when it was pulled off its prey. Chris doesn't remember the cat's scream because blood was pumping against his eardrums and muffled the sounds, but Kim heard it. The scream sounded much like one of her own. She was sure her son was dead, and now the lion was on top of her husband. Chris was on his back, head downslope, stiff arms trying to hold the cougar's fangs away from his face. Back and forth the cat jerked, trying to force its head past those arms. Hind legs clawed for a grip in Chris Brown's legs, and the fangs were inches from his face. With a tremendous heave, Chris threw the cat over himself and 6 feet down the slope, spinning on his back to face the cat again.

Instantly, the lion lunged back at Brown, who appeared defenseless on the ground. Chris met the leap with all the muscle he could put into a kick with both boots. The surprised cougar retreated a step or two. Chris jumped to his feet and grabbed a stick from the ground. It was a frail stick, but Chris brandished it at the cat and brought forth a primitive scream of his own. The cougar hesitated, and then Kim heard the animal scream once more just before it ran into the bushes.

Chris rushed to the boy. A big patch of scalp was missing, apparently swallowed by the lion. Most of the remaining scalp was torn loose. Fang marks scratched the bare skull but the cougar's teeth hadn't penetrated it. A fang or claw had punctured the boy's left cheek. Blood covered David's eyes, and Chris feared at first that the boy's eyes were gone. He grabbed the boy and ran 50 yards back up the trail, where he stopped to wrap his own shirt around David's head to stop the bleeding.

"Am I dead, Dad?" the boy asked.

"Of course not," Chris answered. "You're talking, aren't you? You're just bleeding a little. You've had cuts before. You'll stop bleeding and then you'll be all right again. Say a little prayer with me, and everything will be fine."

They prayed a moment and then Chris picked up his stepson and ran. It would have been shorter to return to park headquarters by continuing on the circular trail in the direction that they had been going, but they thought the lion had gone in that direction, so they backtracked.

Kim kept saying that she heard something moving in the bushes, but Chris told her that there was nothing there in order to keep everyone, especially David, calm.

All the way back, Chris kept David talking so that the boy wouldn't slip into shock and never return. Amazingly, David never cried during the whole ordeal.

Park rangers administered first aid and summoned an ambulance from nearby Alpine, but everyone's troubles were far from over. General practitioner/physiologist Dr. Joanna Sanchez did what she could with the wounds and performed a near miracle in dealing with David's mental attitude. But nobody at Big Bend Memorial Hospital was qualified to initiate surgery on the torn scalp. In David's condition, it was essential that he be quickly moved to a bigger hospital in Dallas.

"We tried to get a local pilot to fly us," Kim recalled later, "but he wanted in the neighborhood of $3,000 or $4,000 in cash before he'd take off. We didn't have it. The police at Alpine told us not to worry and Sergeant Carl Bierman drove the ambulance 600 miles to Dallas. In spite of having to stop three times for gas, he got us there in seven hours!"

Back in the Chisos Mountains, in the big bend of the Rio Grande River, trouble loomed. A mountain lion that had lost its fear of humans and that probably would attack again was running free in the park, which covers almost one million acres. The attack had occurred at about 6 P.M. Anxious to kill the cat before dark, armed rangers fanned out in every direction.

Texas Ranger Clayton McKinney heard about the attack on his radio and at 7:30 P.M. called his nephew, state predator hunter and trapper Bill McKinney, to find out if he had been notified. Bill was stationed in the

100,000-acre Black Gap Wildlife Management Area. (Read more about Bill McKinney's extreme adventures in Chapter 5.) He had been using his hounds in the park's telemetry (radio collar) lion studies. He had also been on call in case there was an emergency need for his dogs. Bill tried to telephone park management, but the phone was busy.

He loaded his hounds in his vehicle, confident that if he got there quickly it would be a short chase. When he reached the park by phone, however, he learned that both the park supervisor and the chief ranger were away. An assistant would pass along Bill's offer of help.

It was 10:30 P.M. when the decision reached him. Bill was told to bring his hounds. By then it was well after dark, and the track was four hours old. It would take at least another hour to reach the attack site. The chance for a short chase had become slim, and a long chase after dark in the steep, rough Chisos Mountains would be dangerous for men and dogs. It would also multiply the chance for mistakes that might permit the lion to escape. The posse agreed to begin the hunt just before daylight the next morning.

Bill asked Doug Waid to join him. Bill had been working with Doug on the lion study and knew that the biologist was tough and wiry and a great help on a lion chase. The pair were in the park before 5 A.M., anxious to begin while it was still cool and moist and before the sun would burn out the scent. But the rangers asked them to wait for their troubleshooter, a climber who rescues people who get trapped on bluffs and in other dangerous situations. His only contribution to this urgent situation was to delay it's resolution. He never showed up.

Other rangers showed up, milled around, and made small talk while they waited. Bill became very anxious. Scent trails do not last forever, and the scent might have been disturbed by searchers the night before. The hounds were not accustomed to crowds, either. Bill feared that they might be distracted and not do their best.

At 6 A.M., Bill was finally permitted to free Missy, one of his two best lion dogs, on the now-twelve-hour-old track at the attack site. Missy showed immediate interest. She made one circle just downhill from the foot trail and raced around the hillside parallel to the trail. She ran in the same direction that the Browns had taken after the attack.

Apparently, Kim Brown had been correct. The lion had not lost interest in its attempted kill, or perhaps it had followed simply because the Browns were running. The predator response is almost always triggered by anything that flees. At any rate, the cougar's trail ran parallel with the Browns' for roughly 150 yards. Finally, the cat track turned 90 degrees away from the foot trail and headed across Laguna Meadow toward a gray-rock foothill in front of 7,000-foot Ward Mountain.

Bill felt a wave of hope. The cat's scent trail was still strong enough for the hounds to follow. Three more hounds were released while Bill and Doug ran through the underbrush toward Missy. The oldest hound, Toby, heard people yelling, thought that he was being called, and ran back to the crowd, where someone tried to catch him. He was spooked out of the race.

Bill and Doug were on their own and climbing as fast as they could. They often slid two steps down for every one they took upward on the loose rock. Feeling that he was halfway up, Bill looked back and saw that he had barely made a good start.

"Doug," he yelled, "get up here with me!"

Doug put on a burst of speed and scrambled up, red-faced and out of breath. "Where are they?" he gasped.

"Out of hearing," Bill answered.

"I thought you yelled that the hounds had treed."

"No," Bill said, "I just want you to stay close to me. If my football knees give out, I can have you take my revolver and go on to kill that cat. You'll have to get in close—right in with the hounds."

"I can do it," Doug assured him, even though he isn't a hunter. "Let's go!"

About halfway up, Bill stopped again. He realized that the chase could have gone out of hearing over the top of the mountain or through a gap called The Window. Right there, the average houndsman would have had a 50/50 chance of choosing the wrong direction and becoming separated from his hounds—perhaps for days. But Bill unpacked his Taconics receiver, which is essentially the same equipment used to track wildlife, and assembled the directional antenna. It's a lot of work and trouble to carry eight pounds of extra equipment on a chase, but there's no better way to locate out-of-hearing hounds. No signal from the radio collars on the hounds came through the gap. This meant that the chase had gone right over the mountain.

After two hours of slipping and sliding, then using their hands to climb, Bill and Doug topped out in a small saddle. The hounds could have gone three ways, but the radio signals told the two men to turn left. Hurrying along the narrow hogback in that direction, the men eventually heard the dog—just before the steady roar of an airplane engine drowned out their barking.

"Damn it!" Doug said. "That plane is supposed to be monitoring radio-collared lions, not us."

They learned later that the radio-collared lions in the basin had left at the first sound of the dogs. Not realizing that they were doing more harm than good, someone had asked the pilot to keep the media informed about the progress of the hunters. Eventually the plane left and, by 11 A.M., the two men were able to catch up with the hounds where the lion had stopped to kill and eat a skunk.

The morning was overcast, which helped prevent the lion's scent trail from completely evaporating, but the strong contrast between skunk scent and the lion trail didn't help. Furthermore, the hounds had climbed fast and were too hot to work effectively. As any good houndsman in the Southwest knows—especially if he hunts desert country—overheating diminishes scenting ability. The men had brought some water, though it's a lot of work to carry it. They poured it into Bill's hat to wet the noses and mouths of the hounds. Somewhat refreshed and with their nasal passages moistened, the hounds trailed into a deep, rough canyon on the back side of the mountain. Once more, the hounds overheated and found trailing difficult. The canteen was empty.

Twice the men found water in the canyon, led the dogs off the track to drink, and then led them back to resume trailing. They also filled the canteen each time to keep the dogs' noses moist. Three times, the hounds couldn't follow at places where the lion had jumped up 12- to 20-foot bluffs. Each time, Doug climbed halfway up and wedged himself in place. Bill passed him the hounds and then Doug drew them over the top. Finally, by helping the hounds through the rugged places, they came to the end of the rocky canyon.

The lion's trail came back to the top of Ward Mountain. It was easier walking, and the hunters hoped for faster trailing. But because the overcast had cleared at about 2 p.m., a warm wind had swept the scent away.

"Water won't help now," Bill told Doug.

He was near desperation. The hounds were tired. The track was blown out, and the day was two-thirds gone.

"We've got to make up some time," Bill told Doug. "My guess is that the cat headed across to the thicker trees around the pour-offs."

The two led all three hounds across the half-mile shortcut, trying not to think about the consequences if they put the dogs onto a new trail that had been made by a different cougar.

Walking instead of trailing did refresh the hounds a little. In minutes, Missy gave voice. Right track or wrong, she was on a lion again. Sam and Rowdy packed in.

The track seemed improved. The bigger, shadier trees and the greater amount of ground vegetation held more moisture and protected the scent from wind and sun. The hounds moved rapidly until they reached the pour-offs, which are rock faces 15 to 20 feet high where rain pours off as it races down a crease in the mountainside. Sometimes the cougar had jumped down or across them in places where the hounds had to be lowered with a rope. That was no real trouble, or there wasn't until the plane returned. Twice more it circled overhead—once for at least

30 minutes. The difficulty of hearing the hounds over the engine noise caused additional delays before the men could find the dogs and lower them down more pour-offs.

Finally, the cat track left the mountain, dropped back down to Laguna Meadow, and headed toward the foot trail less than a quarter mile from the place where David Vaught had been attacked. About 60 yards from the foot trail, Missy gave a surprised *whoo-whoo-whoo* and began barking up a pinyon pine. After twelve hours and seven or eight miles of cold-trailing, a lion was suddenly treed, without even a short jump chase.

Bill cautioned Doug as they approached. Lions sometimes jump out at the sound of human voices. "What do you think, Doug?" Bill whispered. "Is it the right cat?"

"Has to be. Kill it!"

Bill drew his revolver and made a safe lung shot rather than risk wounding the lion and starting another chase with exhausted dogs. The cougar jumped out, ran 200 yards, and climbed a tree again. Bill finished it with a head shot.

The cat was a male estimated to be sixteen to twenty-four months old. He weighed 85 pounds. Proof that this was the right cat came only after prompt work by the Midland, Texas, narcotics laboratory. David's hair was found in the lower intestinal tract. The State Public Health laboratory in El Paso tested the cat's head and found that the cat was not rabid.

That mountain lion would not attack again, but one question would remain unanswered. Why did he do it? The cat was not in poor condition. He did not have a faceful of porcupine quills or any other injury. He was not compelled by any physical disability to seek easy prey. In fact, the cougar wasn't especially hungry. His intestinal contents indicated that he had fed on deer before he ate part of David's scalp.

Perhaps the cougar, because he was born and raised near people in the park, had no fear of human beings. Or maybe he was just an ordinary cat responding instinctively to fleeing prey.

The important question, of course, is: Will it happen again? Because of the sacred cow status granted to park animals by so many people, it seems possible. Some large predators, particularly bears, have lost their fear of human beings in areas where they aren't hunted, and some people have lost their respect for large predators because they have seen too many inaccurate nature films. Both types are found in parks, and trouble seems inevitable.

The rest of the story is about young David. He had four operations and needed at least two more. It would take almost a year and a half before hair would again cover his head. The Dallas Cowboy Cheerleaders heard about his mounting medical bills and gave David a benefit performance.

The night before the performance, David said, "I'm already scared."

"About what?" he was asked.

"Getting up on the stage."

# 3

*People with the survivor personality, Dr. Al Siebert says, find that things go well for them in everyday life as well. Survivor traits help adventurers like Dr. John Sparaga make calm decisions and move with care during the worst emergencies.*

DESCENDING to the snowfield had been a fear-of-falling waking nightmare the entire day. The field's 60-degree slope was the most level surface that Dr. John Sparaga and Ken Alligood had seen since early morning. But now they could actually walk. In comparison to what the men had been through, it seemed as easy as coming down a long flight of stairs . . . until Sparaga's heel hit ice.

As his feet flew forward, the one hundred pounds of Dall sheep meat, cape, and horns he was carrying pulled Sparaga's weight backward. The horns of any other animal would have dug into the snow and slowed him, but this sheep's 41½-inch curls acted as sled runners.

Sparaga accelerated uncontrollably for 100 yards through the fog, certain he'd fly off a cliff. Instead, a rock outcropping loomed into view. The collision would be bruising, but the helpless plummet would at least stop. And then, just before the rocks, Sparaga saw it: a gaping black hole. He was headed right for it.

Because of the Tok Sheep Management Unit's reputation for large Dall sheep, Dr. John Sparaga, a hunter and orthodontist from Anchorage, and his friend Lee Robbins had flown to a strip of gravel near the face of Robertson Glacier, north of the Wrangell Mountains in the Alaska

Range. Mountaineer Ken Alligood had come along for the climb. After quickly setting up a base camp, the trio strapped on 80-pound packs and hiked up the glacier's 20-degree face. Carrying a tent and freeze-dried food, they planned to camp wherever the end of each day's hunt found them.

Two miles up, they spotted a magnificent patriarch and several lesser rams. The big fellow had spotted them as well. First he stepped out to watch them, then he slipped back into the protection of a hole carved into the ridge. At the slightest hint of danger, the big sheep could disappear out the back of the hole and make his escape down the other side of the ridge.

For the hunters, the only approach was up a 2,000-foot cut in the face of the mountain. Most of the bottom half was a loose 60- to 70-degree shale slide. The men would be scrambling on their hands and feet all the way up. Above that, the cut was steeper. The climb didn't seem worth the risk.

For the next six days, the group kept seeing sheep farther up the glacier, but every other animal paled in comparison to the magnificent ram they had seen on the first day. Back where they had started, Lee Robbins settled for a lesser ram halfway down from the patriarch's hole. Sparaga could only watch as, repeatedly, the big ram stepped out to feed on browned vegetation, looked at them, then ducked back into the hole. "Ken," Sparaga finally said, "it probably gets worse up there than it looks from here, but it's our last day. I'm ready to try climbing above him. Let's worry about the rest if we get there."

Alligood, the experienced mountaineer, had no fears for himself. With soft-soled rock-climbing shoes and 50 feet of 7/16-inch nylon marine rope wound around his waist, he was ready to go. Sparaga would not be as agile in his big-lugged leather boots, but he was determined.

When the ram ducked back into his hole at 8 A.M. on their last day, Sparaga and Alligood took off. Hiding behind ridges and rocks when the sheep came out, they scrambled up the shale.

Above the loose rock and into the deeper, narrower stretch of the cut, a ridge kept them better hidden from the ram's view. Toe holes could be kicked into the snow, which had not thawed at this elevation.

Five hours after starting, they had ascended 2,000 feet. There was even a saddle in the ridge to cross over and get above the ram. Sparaga looked down. The patriarch was about 100 yards below, chewing his cud. Just as Sparaga's crosshairs found the animal, it heard something, stood and looked up. "Shoot!" Alligood hissed urgently.

Sparaga fired. The ram dropped, then jumped back up and ran 10 feet onto a ledge. He was about to leap off into space when another shot from Sparaga stopped him permanently.

Strapping meat, cape, and horns onto his backpack, Sparaga looked at a snowfield they had not been able to see before. "Ken, I can't make it back down the way we came. If we can get over there, it couldn't be as bad."

Blocking the snowfield were 20- to 40-foot vertical ridgebacks, carved in relief against the rock wall like the tall, narrow pipes of a giant church organ. The only possible descent was down the vertical grooves between the ridges. Once committed, the men would have no way back up. The chutes were wet and slick, with snowmelt pouring over some to shoot off in waterfalls at the bottom.

Alligood braced his feet against small protrusions of rock at the top of the first chute to lower Sparaga by rope. If Ken lost his footing and had to let go, John would bounce all the way to the bottom—500 yards below.

Sparaga felt the heavy backpack trying to pull him off the mountain, but somehow he made it to a tiny ledge. Now Alligood wound the rope around his waist and spidered his way down the chute backwards, gripping cracks and 1- or 2-inch protrusions of rock.

The series of chutes was becoming impassable. Perhaps the going would be easier farther over. Carefully creeping along the narrow ledges and around the corners of rocks, the two men found themselves blocked by another vertical ridge. There was no choice but to go back and continue down. They encountered a second chute. And another.

And another. Finally they faced the fifth, the last and worst. Snowmelt flowed freely in the 40-foot cut.

Sparaga went over the edge, slipping and sliding. Hanging like a puppet, he had no way to maneuver himself out of the water. The rope dragged and scrapped rocks loose to shower onto his head and shoulders.

At last, Sparaga approached the bottom. But instead of hitting a ledge, his feet were dangling in a waterfall. Alligood kept lowering him into the shower. Finally, with almost no rope to spare, Sparaga's boots touched rock. Though drenched and cold, he could walk out of the waterfall onto rock. The 800-yard snowfield was nearby.

Traveling through the field was uneventful for the first 200 yards. But it was now 7 P.M. Sparaga was fatigued from 11 hours of climbing, and his backpack load felt twice as heavy as it had before. And now, without warning, his feet left the mountain and the slide toward the black hole began.

Slamming against the far wall of the hole, he bounced back and forth before jolting to a stop 25 feet below the surface of the snowfield. The air smelled dank. Far beneath him were gurgling sounds—an underground river. Gingerly, Sparaga reached out with his left foot. Nothing. But his right foot touched a wall. He was hanging! Careful not to jostle and dislodge himself, he reached back with his left hand and touched ice. His right hand touched rock.

This, Sparaga reasoned, is the snowfield melting out from under itself like a glacier. That stream below would likely disappear into the mountain and never emerge. He looked up and saw light. Amazed, Sparaga realized he was hanging by the ram's horns strapped on his back. Their spread was too wide to fit through the narrow part of the funnel. Of course, a wrong move could make one horn shift and slide up, forcing the other one down. Then the horns would unstoppably side-slip down the hole that, Sparaga's feet had already discovered, widened directly below him.

Almost afraid to breathe, Sparaga called, "Ken! Are you up there?" Silence.

Twenty seconds later, Ken called back, "John! You down there?"

"Yeah, I need a rope. And belay it well. I have to work myself free. Be careful. I hear water below me. If I slip off, I'm gone."

John could hear rope slapping the wall as it descended. Barely moving, he held a hand out until he touched the rope. With slow, smooth motions, he tied it to the rail at the top of his backpack.

Alligood reeled in some rope, belayed it with a turn around his waist, and jammed his feet against the rocks beyond the rim of the hole. He couldn't pull Sparaga directly out, but if John could create slack, Alligood could take it up by quickly pulling the rope around his waist, and in this way the desperate orthodontist could be worked upward. Sparaga braced both feet against the narrowest part of the funnel, pushed up, and freed the horns. Ken took up the slack. Another push, and the hole became too wide for Sparaga's legs to span. Kicking and grabbing against one side or the other, he lunged upward. Alligood responded to each lunge by quickly taking in another inch or two of rope.

Close to the top Sparaga couldn't kick across the hole. But Alligood was pulling hard against the rope on the downhill side. By facing downhill Sparaga was dragged against the wall, where he found grips here and there for his hands and knees.

After an exhausting half-hour struggle, Sparaga emerged. His knees were severely injured. Nevertheless, in the dark, he and Alligood felt their way down until the mountain bellied out to a better slope. It was 11 P.M.

Two hours later they walked into base camp. In the warmth of a big fire, John checked his knees. Shreds of flesh hung from the cuts he'd suffered during the tense struggle up the rocky hole. Sparaga found his first-aid kit, cleaned the wounds, and sutured them—ten stitches each—without anesthetic.

It was easy to imagine that the ram he killed was trying to kill him in return. But in fact Dr. John Sparaga would have died in that hole had he not challenged the mountain for its best set of horns.

# 4

*When a nuisance alligator that should have been an easy 15-minute catch turned into one cliffhanger after another, trapper Curtis Lucas invented a solution for each new challenge.*

LUCAS, thirty, looked into the 30-inch corrugated steel drainage culvert and saw a single alligator eye. Good! This would be the dog-and-cat-eating troublemaker he had been asked to hunt down. Florida alligators grow to 12 feet and 550 pounds, but this one was rumored to be closer to 6 feet. Just two weeks before, Curtis had survived a tussle with an 11-footer that had bitten five holes in his aluminum boat. This job, he thought, would be easy in comparison. He'd go get his coonhunter's headlamp and hatchet and then chase the alligator down to the catch basin, where it could be dispatched.

Curtis didn't see the eye again when he looked into the culvert a second time, but farther down was a dark form that appeared to be the back of the alligator's head. A trickle of water was in the bottom of the pipe, so he pulled off his boots to keep them dry and slid in, crawling on his hands and knees. Soon, however, Curtis began to feel a little leery. This gator wasn't running like he was supposed to. Well, he thought, I have the hatchet, and there's enough room to bring it down hard in a pipe this size. If push comes to shove, I'll hammer him in the head. But with 15 feet to go, Curtis slowed to an alert, nervous creep.

The culvert was 80 yards from the entrance to the catch basin. It formed part of a drainage and water-holding system for a parking lot in an elite housing development six miles from Port Orange, complete with golf course, runway, and airplane hangars behind many of the houses. The runoff flowed from catch basins into a holding pond used to water the golf course.

When Curtis had gone for his gear, he had asked his longtime friend and helper Henry Saul, sixty, to take the .357-caliber bang stick to the catch basin and be ready to slide it through the iron grate and hit the gator in the head as soon as it appeared. Bang sticks were originally used by divers to kill sharks. This one had a 4-foot length of conduit for a handle bolted to the power head. The chamber screwed on. The base plate had a fixed firing pin and was threaded to receive the chamber that held the cartridge. The chamber was about 1/8 inch longer than the cartridge. Once it was screwed down, the firing pin was about 1/16 inch from the primer. A little spring held the firing pin away from the primer until you hit something with it. Then it fired, and the bullet went into whatever you hit.

While Henry was going to the catch basin with the bang stick, Curtis was inching toward the dark form. He was 12 feet away, and it still refused to run. He wished he could stand up for a better look, but kept inching along, expecting all hell to break loose any second. He was within 10 feet, and then about 8 feet away, and even at this low angle, his headlamp clearly illuminated the dark form. It was a hunk of rock.

"Henry!?" He didn't have to yell. Voices travel along the culvert walls, and it sounds as if the person you're talking to is at your elbow.

"Yeah?"

"Has the gator come down yet?"

"Nope, I haven't seen him."

"Well, I saw his eye in the pipe, and I know I didn't crawl over him, and he's not between me and you, so I'm coming down for a look."

That meant moving another 60 yards, and it took a while. It was a hot June day, dank and humid in the culvert, and Curtis was dripping sweat long before he arrived. But the puzzle was solved.

"Henry, I'm looking straight across this basin and there's a smaller pipe, 24 inches I think, and it travels right in line with this one. Hey, there's sand in the bottom, and I see footprints and a tail drag. Do you see anything about another 80 yards in that direction?"

"Yeah, another grate."

"I can see light down there. Go have a look and see if it's a dead end, or if it turns off in another direction."

In a few moments Henry said in a normal voice, as if they were side by side, "It's a dead end."

"Okay, the plan is still good. He's between us now. You wait with the bang stick, and I'll chase him to you."

The bottom of the smaller culvert, being about a foot higher than the larger one, had drained, so the sand in it was dry and sharp. Curtis shoved his 5-foot, 11-inch, 190-pound frame into that 24-inch corrugated pipe, but it was too tight for him to crawl. He moved along like an inchworm, pulling with his elbows against the corrugations and pushing with his toes. Several inches with each pull was the best he could do. His shoulders grazed the sides and his headlamp banged the top every time he raised his head. Holding the lamp in his hand helped. The hatchet was in his other hand, but he couldn't raise it high enough to deliver a blow powerful enough to stop the alligator. Turning around and retreating was out of the question.

Curtis became apprehensive. He thought, "I'm far enough down this pipe that I should have heard the bang stick go off by now. If Henry hasn't yet seen the gator, chances are it beat him to the end, turned around and is headed back."

That boosted the threat level dramatically. Crowding an alligator backwards is far more difficult and dangerous than trying to frighten it into going forward.

"If I have to, maybe I can poke him off with the hatchet," Curtis thought. "And I'll make myself fill the pipe and look more threatening so I can crowd him until his natural instincts make him want to back away."

Satisfied with his plan, Curtis inched along as quickly as possible. And there was the alligator, eyes shining back at the headlamp. It was holding its ground, never mind that Curtis filled the pipe. Curtis was getting too close for comfort, and still the gator wouldn't budge. Not until Curtis was up on his elbows within 10 feet and still coming did it back up a bit. And it was angry about it. It hissed. Curtis hissed back and kept crowding. He couldn't stop and let the alligator regroup. They were nearing the catch basin when somehow the gator's tail got bent back toward Curtis. The alligator appeared to be wedged in the culvert. Curtis still kept inching forward. There was now 7 feet between them.

At 6 feet, the gator lost its nerve, somehow got its tail straightened out, and backed into the basin.

Curtis saw Henry lowering the bang stick and suddenly realized that a .357 firing that close, and in the pipe, was sure to deafen him. Earlier he had assumed he'd be only a short way into the culvert when Henry banged the alligator. Curtis dropped his light and hatchet and quickly stuck fingers in his ears.

Henry banged the gator in the head, but the bang stick misfired. Being hit spooked the alligator—and gators are very fast over short distances. Curtis had just enough time to stick his hands out, palms up. The gator ran right into them, and Curtis had it by the nose. It flipped and flopped and at one point broke free, because Curtis was on his belly with his arms stretched out. In such a position, he couldn't use his body strength to fight with.

"It's going to get my hands in those jaws," Curtis thought. "I've got to think of a better way."

But there was no other option at the moment. He continued sparring with the gator until he caught the nose. Now the creature was trying to roll. Curtis's arms could only twist so far before the alligator broke free. Fortunately, the culvert being as small as it was, the gator would start to roll up one side, so as soon as Curtis was at about his breaking point it would fall off, without making a full roll. It would then repeat that action on the other side. Curtis was able to hang on until the alligator exhausted itself and stopped trying to roll.

Curtis got a better grip on the nose and called up to Henry, "I've got him caught and under control now. Pull off that grate. I'll shove him down there, and we'll take him out of the pipe."

"It can't be lifted out," Henry called back. "They laid the grate when the concrete was wet, and it sank in before the cement dried."

"Get the ax from the truck and bust the concrete around edge of the grate. You'll be able to lift it out."

Henry was back promptly, but every time he whacked that cemented grate it spurred the alligator into a fit of wild flopping.

"Henry, stop. I can't hold on much longer."

"What now?" Curtis thought. "I need a better way to hold this gator than by the nose with my arms stretched out front. Wonder if I could pull him under me and hold his jaws shut with the weight of my body."

Curtis dragged the jaws under his chest, but not very far, because his shoulders were now pressed against the sides of the culvert and the pipe prevented his elbows from extending far enough out for his upper arms to swivel in his shoulder joints. With the beast's nose pinned under his chest, he scooted forward just enough to grab onto its tail. With his torso over the jaws, he could now keep both ends of the alligator immobile.

"Okay, Henry, I got him secured."

Henry took another good whack at the concrete, and the ax broke.

"Henry, we're down to our last option. I'll scoot back and get the gator by the nose again and push it under the grate. We'll have to hope that the bang stick goes off this time and doesn't blow my eardrums."

By now the easy 15-minute job Curtis had expected had turned into a cliffhanger that had attracted an audience interested in seeing how it would end. One spectator offered to go home for his .22 if that would help. It sure would. The muzzle could be shoved through the grate nearly to the gator's head, and the report wouldn't rupture Curtis' eardrums.

Curtis was ready with the alligator when the man returned with the gun. Henry popped the gator, but of course reptiles don't catch on right away that they're dead, so Curtis now struggled with an alligator that could fight as well dead as it could alive.

"Henry, pass your knife down here."

With the long and very sharp blade, Curtis cut through the spine, and that ended it. Almost.

"We still have to get that grate off, Henry. It's not possible to pull that gator behind me in this little pipe, and I don't have it left in me to push it ahead for 160 yards."

A heroine stepped forward. "I'll hook a chain to my four-wheel-drive and yank that grate right off of there."

It took several jerks, but finally the grate flew loose from the concrete. Curtis passed the alligator up to Henry. The heroine didn't leave her name or wait around for thanks. But Curtis made a promise to her, to himself, and to anybody else in the world who might have been interested: He would never again crawl in a pipe with an alligator. Though he has had the opportunity since, it is one resolution he has not broken.

# 5

*Jack Kilpatric didn't have time to think, but he "knew" what to do to save ol' Sam—punch that lion in the nose.*

"WE USED TO joke about hunting in Big Bend National Park," grinned Jack Kilpatric. "If we could only turn our hounds loose down there, we'd say, we couldn't shoot fast enough to kill all the lions our dogs would tree.

"Now here we were two days into a hunt in the best lion range of the Chisos Mountains, and we couldn't cut a track."

"It turned out like most lion hunts," said Bill McKinney. "Just boredom for days, and then complete terror."

McKinney is a sort of hired gun in the Black Gap Wildlife Management Area in southwestern Texas. Among his many duties is keeping the mountain lions and coyotes down to manageable numbers. For years, the 800,000 acres of high desert that make up the Black Gap WMA have been a restoration site for the rare desert bighorn sheep. Next door is Big Bend National Park, a million acres cradled in a vast curve of the Rio Grande River. It contains the beautiful Chisos Mountains—prime cougar habitat.

McKinney was not only invited to hunt the park: he was also being paid. Biologist Doug Waid was doing a lion study, and the simplest, most cost-effective way of putting telemetry collars on cats is to catch them with hounds and dart them. You leave the guns at home, of course. And that's what eventually made the terror complete.

Kilpatric also works for Texas Parks and Wildlife, as area manager for the Elephant Mountain WMA, and had long been involved in keeping lions out of Black Gap's sheep pasture. Lion eradication had never been the intent, of course. It was simply a matter of limiting predation of these "high dollar" sheep and other wildlife in the management area.

Like McKinney and most other good houndsmen, Kilpatric does not see the kill as a hunt's highest purpose. Hunting to support a scientific investigation of one of his favorite animals offered a far greater challenge. Kilpatric jumped at the opportunity to go along, eager to see all those lions running like rabbits in every direction.

Two days without a bark hadn't reduced the challenge, but it did necessitate a fateful change. If the lions weren't in the best range, maybe they were in the worst. On the third day, the hounds were put down in the Grapevine Hills, a two-mile-wide string of boulder piles that McKinney describes as "leftovers from building the Chisos Mountains."

Kilpatric was riding McKinney's little black Mexican cow pony that day. He was even dressed, McKinney claimed, for a ride in the park— right down to his leather gloves. McKinney and Waid were on foot. As they entered the mouth of a canyon, several javelinas ran out, and expectations rose dramatically. A lion could loaf for days around the springs at the bottom of this canyon, eating any javelinas that ventured in for water.

The hounds soon verified this speculation, but the scent was old— just a touch here and there. Scrapes had been made by a male lion, and the animal had gone up a slickrock pour-off where water cascades downward during a rain. Lots of odor was left where the cougar had killed a ringtail cat, but no ground scent could be trailed in a definite direction.

Missy, the red-and-white matriarch of the pack, switched to checking bushes. Most of the vegetation was strong-smelling greasewood, difficult shrubbery to trail through. But now and again she boo-hooed that a lion had brushed against a branch.

Gradually, Missy worked the pack through to where the scent turned into a decent running track.

Two other dogs, Rowdy and Toby, gave voice and trailed out of the canyon. Kilpatric rode ahead, trying to cut sign to speed up the chase. In minutes, a weird-sounding new dog was yelping.

Waid's jaw dropped. "What's that?"

"That's Jack," McKinney grinned. "He runs silent when he's cutting trail. He doesn't open unless it's a jump track, so he's looking at that lion. Let's get to him!"

The dogs caught on as well. They passed Kilpatric and connected with the mountain lion's body-scent funnel. Cougars are fast sprinters, but they don't have the lungs for a long chase. This one made it another 400 yards up the approach to the mountain, but there wasn't a tree anywhere. He stopped to face the dogs on a broken-rock ridge. Some rocks were bigger than the cab of a pickup truck. The ridge was a giant jumbled mess that made horseback riding impossible.

Kilpatric dismounted. It's dangerous enough when a lion is bayed on the ground. The hounds get too close to its fangs and claws. Furthermore, when the man with the gun arrives, dogs become extra brave, assuming they're safer. The hounds didn't know that Kilpatric's sidearm was at home today. Waid had a tranquilizer gun, but serum puts a lion down slowly. All three men needed to be there when the dogs rushed the cougar. Kilpatric waited nervously.

The moment McKinney and Waid caught up, Kilpatric raced across the rocks. McKinney noticed the rope leashes still tied to the saddle. They would be needed to tie the dogs back so they wouldn't hurt the tranquilized cat. He stopped long enough to grab them and arrived at the uproar several steps behind Kilpatric.

The lion was on the far, lower edge of a huge flat tilted rock. All five dogs were above the cougar, screaming in its face—and in danger of sliding into the beast. The instant Kilpatric appeared, the hounds piled onto the lion, whose haunches slid off the table rock and into a hole formed by other rocks. That left Sam standing on the backs of two dogs and barking behind the cougar's ear. The cat spun around, hooked a thumb-claw into Sam's leg, and flipped him back up on the table rock. The dog landed on his side with his back toward the feline, which promptly ripped a 5-inch patch of his hide loose.

Kilpatric jumped onto the table rock, running at the lion to kick it off Sam. "Bill," he yelled, "you'd better get here and help me. We're about to lose some dogs." Just in time Kilpatric realized that a running kick would leave him sliding on one foot down the slick, slanted rock—right into the jaws of the cat. He stopped short as the cougar opened its mouth to bite again at Sam's spine. With no weapon and no time to think, Kilpatric dropped to the lion's level, braced himself against sliding with his left hand, and threw a hard right cross straight into the cougar's nose, snapping its head back. The lion's eyes lit up like copper burning green in hot fire. Its muscles bunched, and Kilpatric knew the cat was about to leap right over the dogs to get to him. Just then Sam recaptured the lion's attention by trying to wriggle free.

McKinney joined the fracas about the time Kilpatric yelled for help. Missy was trying to scratch her way onto the table rock to join the fight. McKinney ran up behind the lion and snatched Missy before she got caught. He quickly tried to grab more hounds, all the while yelling, "Doug! Shoot that son of a gun!"

The lion was again attempting to bite Sam in the spine. But this time his eyes were on Kilpatric as he slowly lowered his head toward the dog. Kilpatric scooted a tad closer, yelled "H-a-a-a-h-h!," and hammered his fist down hard on top of the lion's head.

The cat's head instantly bounced back up away from the dog, and fury again glowed green in its eyes. Missy pulled free and ran back, trying to get killed in an attempt to rescue Kilpatric and Sam. Not wanting her to escalate this dangerous mess any further, and still yelling for Waid to shoot, McKinney once more snatched Missy away from the cougar. This time, it was McKinney and Missy's commotion that drew the lion's attention away from Kilpatric.

Focusing entirely on the lion, neither Kilpatric nor McKinney knew exactly where Waid was or what he was doing. But they did know the cougar wasn't acting drugged. "Doug, shoot! Shoot the lion!"

"I did!" Waid finally yelled back.

There had been room for Waid to aim the tranquilizer gun at the lion's hip when McKinney first yanked Missy out of that hole. The serum hadn't had a chance to work yet.

Before the lion went under, Sam tried to squirm away. The 135-pound lion grabbed the dog by the back and shook him violently. Kilpatric slugged the cat in the head once more, knocking the two animals apart.

Hot green eyes riveted back on Kilpatric. Muscles bunched. But for the third time, Kilpatric was saved. Two hounds that McKinney had not yet caught piled onto the rock, challenging the cat. Sam escaped.

Knowing that the drug was finally taking effect on the lion, McKinney reached in the hole and grabbed Rowdy. As the lion faded out, it now became a job of protecting the cat from the dogs. Even Sam tried to jump back into the hole with the cat when it slumped off the table rock.

Finally, in a tangle of ropes, all of the dogs were caught. Waid took scientific data and installed the radio telemetry collar on the cougar's neck. It was a tough old tom that had suffered a broken tail and numerous battle scars from territorial fights with other males.

McKinney looked at Kilpatric, the other tough old tom, and tried to think of something nice to say about his friend's heroic performance. "Dang it, Jack," he said. "You're gonna have to improve your manners if you're gonna help collar cats in the Big Bend. Look at this animal! Its nose is bleeding and you loosened its front tooth! If you want to hunt with me, no more hittin' around on these park lions."

Kilpatric didn't let all those compliments go to his head. At that moment he was just very pleased that his three rounds with the lion had ended in a draw.

(To read more about Bill's and Waid's extreme adventures, see Chapter 2.)

# 6

*Rescue is highly satisfying, adventurous work, but for many reasons, not everybody wants it as a career. Out of every thirty to forty who do, and take a "pass test" to qualify for a para-rescueman class, an average of only 10 percent make it. A figure that low suggests that few of us don't fall apart when we're suddenly and unexpectedly stripped of our accustomed support system.*

JIM MUNSON, forty-one, owner of Alaska's SouthCentral Air, opened his eyes to the black Casio watch still running on his wrist. 12:43 A.M.

12:43! A moment ago, Munson remembered with returning horror, the lights went out on Sparrevohn's airstrip. But that moment ago was actually 11:10 A.M. God, the wind blowing through here is cold. Don't remember the crash. Must have been out for an hour and a half. Steve looks like he's still out. Sleeping maybe.

Munson reached over to awaken his co-pilot. No response. Is he breathing? Oh, God, there's blood in his ears and nose. The pulse. Jim touched Steve's neck, his fingers too cold to feel anything. He blew on his hand and tried again. Agonizingly, he tried yet again before admitting that Steven Walters, thirty-four, was cold and stiffened beyond help.

Jim found what was left of his headset and tried to radio a distress signal. Dead.

Maybe it was less windy in the cargo area. Trying to get up, Munson realized what had slammed a bend in the control yoke that holds the pilot's wheel. His body. Something was seriously wrong with his left leg, left shoulder, right ribs, and right ankle. Barely able to crawl out of his seat, Munson ignored the pain as best he could and dragged himself out of the cockpit. Piling coats and sleeping bags over himself, he was determined to ward off hypothermia as long as possible. He was reasonably certain that no timely mountain rescue attempt was possible in the terrifying turbulence that threw his deHavilland Caribou out of the air.

Max, traffic controller at the Anchorage Air Control Center, saw the green blip fall off his radar screen. Never identified by more than that friendly first name, he'd been calling out altitudes and weather data as Munson's Caribou descended from 10,000 feet in a powered glide toward Sparrevohn's dangerous daytime-only, one-way airstrip. There were no runway lights. Located on the slope of a mountain with its entrance end lowest, the strip terminated against a ridge. Miss the first try, and you died.

Munson had requested an instrument approach with a vector to the final approach. Not available. A visual approach was his only choice, and all Munson could see was a pair of portable flashing strobe lights at the runway entrance. Yet with one engine out, the other backfiring, and no other human habitation within 133 miles, he couldn't fly on. He had aimed at the lights through his windshield, slowed his speed to 63 knots, and started down.

Max became nervous. "Do you know you're below 5,800 feet?

'Yes," Munson shot back, "5,800 feet and descending. Runway end lights in view." Moments later: "Center! We have lost runway end lights. Have Sparrevohn turn them back on, or we're sunk!"

And the green blip disappeared, replaced by the beeps of an Emergency Locator Transmitter beacon. Immediately, Max called the 210th Rescue Squadron at Kulis Air National Guard Base, Anchorage. Crews and para-rescuemen (PJs) from an HC-130 Kingbird and an HH-60 helicopter had just gotten home—tired from training flights—when they were scrambled back for the real thing.

Jim Munson sat shivering under his covering, filled with a terror of hypothermia he'd picked up twenty-nine years earlier. At that time his parents had been so engaged in a bitter breakup, so completely occupied with their own personal hate and anger, that nothing was left for the children but emotional demolition. Jim would show them. He dashed from the house in jeans and sneakers, determined to hide the night in a cavity he dug in a pile of snow. Soon Jim was shaking uncontrollably, but he wouldn't budge. Let them see how they made him suffer. Nobody came looking. Nobody even noticed his absence. And then, in the final stage of hypothermia, he began to feel strangely warm. The abnormality of this awakened strong survival instincts, and he staggered back inside.

"Inside" was now his shattered aircraft, with 10-below winds whipping through cracks and holes. His shivering would soon give way to abnormal warmth, and again, he thought, nobody would come.

Jumpmaster Mike Drummond, who lived the farthest from Kulis, got the message to scramble as soon as he opened the door. After nearly nineteen years, ninety-six saves, and many, many less-life-threatening missions, he still considered it no imposition, no inconvenience, to launch again after a long day.

Drummond's life had found its focus when he was in the seventh grade, when he was assigned to write a list of what he intended to accomplish from that moment through adulthood. By graduation, only certain details had changed. Classmates were going to work for Zippo or Corning in western Pennsylvania. But he had thought all along that life should be a satisfying adventure, perhaps like "Rampart Squad 51," which he watched on TV in the early 1970s. The Allegheny National Forest had been his backyard. Now he wanted to jump from airplanes, scuba dive, climb mountains. And maybe the adventures would be more satisfying if he was a military para-rescueman.

Military honors, awards, and medals would soon become meaningless, but making a difference—cheating death out of a victim against incredible odds—was immeasurably satisfying. Now, having received the order to scramble, he hurried to the Rescue Coordination Center at Fort Richardson Army Base, Anchorage, for the mission briefing.

The pager caught paramedic John Loomis at home reading. He, too, was tired, but eager to go. After fifteen years, he could still say, "Missions are fun. If we didn't have practice alerts to keep us occupied, we'd be fighting each other to get on the real missions." His favorite story was of a Canadian search-and-rescue tech who was being praised by a woman who'd been saved after a plane crash. "Mum," said the rescuer, "if it wasn't for rent and groceries, we'd do this for free."

Loomis trained in a big class of eight. Most classes have five trainees. It starts, however, with forty to sixty people taking the "pass test." It's a weeding process to single out those who are themselves survivors, those who have what psychologist Dr. Al Siebert has defined as the survivor trait. These are people who don't fall apart when they're suddenly, unexpectedly stripped of their accustomed support system. In fact, they are constantly challenging themselves in new circumstances, which explains why they see dangerous missions as fun. They think on their feet, make the best use of whatever is at hand, and, most important, they are adjustable. If something isn't working, they try something else. And they continue readjusting their thinking until something does work. Having the survivor trait as part of your personality is a prerequisite for starting training.

Guilt crept in, adding mental torment to Munson's physical injuries. Why Steve? He had the best reason not to die. With 1,700 hours as a B-52 captain, he had joined SouthCentral Air as a pilot/mechanic just so he could learn to fly small planes under the most extreme conditions. He and his wife were planning a life as flying overseas missionaries.

Munson's eyes fell on the last piece of cargo they were to deliver—the 5,300-pound air compressor—and recalled the last moments of terror.

They were in the powered glide. Moments later, they were at 5,000 feet and suddenly slammed by wildly turbulent 50-knot winds that nobody knew about. Whipping over and around mountaintops, the tremendous gusts tossed the heavily laden Caribou about the sky like a leaf. He felt the plane shoot straight up and straight down, and once it was thrown tail-first. Seat belts bit across the pilots' hips as the plane plummeted. The next moment they were rammed into their seats by G forces. Lord, Munson thought, we're upside down, looking at Sparrevohn's runway end lights through the cockpit's ceiling window!

The huge air compressor located under the center section of the wings groaned against its harness. If something let go, the falling compressor could have taken out both wings. The Caribou righted itself. But air speed was now below stall. Jim had to get the engine back up to climb power. And at that precarious moment, the runway end lights went black. Damn it! Jim thought. They don't want us to land! Actually, the plane had been thrown behind a ridge.

Landing gear and flaps back up, Jim shoved the throttle forward. He remembered no more, but now he realized what had happened. Wind gusting from behind at nearly the same speed as the plane had left the craft with almost no actual air speed. No air speed, no lift. It's called wind shear. The Caribou fell, pancaking onto the mountain.

With all pilots, crew, and PJs assembled, Mike Drummond felt a familiar discomfort about the unfolding plan. Early in his career, he had been told that children were aboard a downed plane. The plane had hit bad weather, failed to clear a 10,000-foot mountain by 100 feet, and crashed onto a hanging glacier just above where the glacier "calves." The tail hung over a 1,500-foot drop-off. Above the plane was a huge fracture in the glacier, probably widened by the crash.

Hovering over the site, the rescuers could find no signs of life and had to abandon the mission as far too dangerous to attempt to retrieve bodies. Drummond, already troubled because he, too, had children, became deeply disturbed when the bereaved family criticized him for not taking the risk. From that moment, Drummond was driven to find logical ways to improve the outcome possibilities of every rescue, while still insisting on team safety. An injured rescuer is useless to the victim and requires care himself.

On this night, the plan called for two PJs on the helicopter and two more on the HC-130. "If the chopper does get through," Drummond suggested, "we'll jump one man from the Kingbird."

"Why?" asked Major Victor Evans, acting Search and Rescue Director for this mission.

"Because otherwise I may have only one qualified paramedic taking care of two people all the way back to Anchorage."

Realizing that the same thing would happen if the chopper didn't get through, Major Evans made a fateful decision. "We'll put three PJs on the HC-130. When we get to Kulis, draw names to see who from the helicopter goes on the Kingbird."

Eight-year rescue veteran Sergeant John Paff "won" the drawing. Paff was exposed to the para-rescue virus at fifteen while just starting a professional water-skiing career at Cypress Gardens, Florida. A rescue squadron was there doing Memorial Day demonstration jumps, and Paff was befriended by a twenty-one-year-old named Jim. They corresponded for a time, and Jim suggested Paff become a PJ. "I have other aspirations," he answered.

It wasn't until he was out of high school and not doing especially well in college that Paff did consider it an option. When he tried to contact Jim again, he learned his friend had died doing low-level water training in a helicopter at night. The pilot of the craft thought he was hovering, but instead was slowly moving backwards. The tail dipped into the water. The chopper spun and crashed, killing all but two. Paradoxically, this actually drew Paff deeper into learning what rescue was all about. The more he learned, the more interesting it seemed.

He rarely says it, but today Paff is very aware that when a victim is in a life-threatening situation, nobody is more important to him than the rescue team. It's a heavy responsibility, but the job is tremendously rewarding when a life is saved.

And so it was that Paff won the drawing.

Taking off ahead of the Kingbird, the chopper was driven back by icing and poor visibility 15 minutes into the flight. They'd never make it through the Lake Clark pass visually, nor could they fly over the 10,000-foot mountains in the crew's 30-minute allowable time limit for safety at that altitude.

The Kingbird could fly over the mess at 24,000 feet. Although its crew was also dealing with sporadic icing and was flying on instruments, they were circling the Caribou's last known location in 90 minutes. But where was the crash? Even through infrared night-vision goggles, no wreckage could be seen.

Flight Engineer Sergeant Jeff Ullom checked his watch. It was 1:30 A.M. The Caribou had gone down almost two-and-a-half hours earlier. If anyone was still alive, hypothermia would be threatening in a serious way. "We might speed things up with an illumination flare," Ullom suggested. "Some crews are reporting real enhancement using flares and goggles together."

The moment the flare ignited, co-pilot Captain Peter Katinszky spotted the Caribou.

The old knot from the glacier wreck once more hit the pit of Drummond's stomach. This was clearly not a survivable crash. The nose was damaged, the wings were torn and twisted off, and the fuselage was split in two. The battered tail section hung partially over the edge of the small "bench" where the plane had pancaked. To jump in the 50-knot turbulence that had thrown this powered plane out of the air—to take such a risk to retrieve bodies—was absolutely out of the question.

Jim Munson alerted to a faint, distant hum. That sound in the dead silence of the wintry wilderness was immediately unmistakable. An aircraft! Munson dug under his coat, where he had shoved a little Mini-Mag flashlight to keep its tiny AA cells warm. He harbored no hope that a rescue was being attempted, but maybe this pilot would notice his small light and report the location. As the sound grew to an overhead roar, Munson waved his beam though every crack and hole in the smashed plane. The aircraft flew by and swung back, and suddenly the sky lit up, bright as day. It was a rescue! Munson waved his beam with a vengeance.

John Paff, wearing the goggles, suddenly shouted, "I see a light flashing!"

"Where? Where?" his teammates asked.

Then everybody saw it. Life! Drummond knew they'd find a way to jump. The enthusiasm was dampened by a suggestion that the plane might have been on fire, but Paff didn't think it was. "The goggles make the flashes glow, but it's not flickering like fire."

The flares they dropped were being blown for miles before hitting ground, so jumping directly to the Caribou remained out of the question. Captain Katinszky remembered that there was a wind meter on the ridge, and a radio call to Sparrevohn verified that gusts were exceeding 50 knots. However, up higher, and at the airstrip a few miles to the east, winds were almost half that at 2,000 feet and only 10 knots at ground level. The Kingbird couldn't land without running lights, but it could make a pass at 2,000 feet and not risk hitting the mountain where the airstrip ends.

Initial winds exceeded the 22-knot practice jump limit, but PJs are not restricted on missions. A small, weighted spotter chute with strobe lights was dropped to estimate fall and drift rates. Drummond picked the jump point using the headlights of a tracked military vehicle called a Small Unit Support Vehicle, or SusV, as the target. Even with 27-mile forward speed generated by their rectangular canopies, the wind blew the jumpers backwards until they dropped to 100 feet, but the calculations were accurate. Loomis landed just in front of the headlights, and the other two off to the sides.

Captain Toy Owen, pilot, brought the Kingbird back over the dead-end ridge and aimed at the runway entrance in order to fly low enough to accurately drop the medical equipment, plus enough survival gear to last the PJs three days. Drummond had told Task Sergeant Kirk Whitehurst, "Be accurate. We can't waste time searching." With only the SusV's headlights, and seconds to see where to drop, Whitehurst also had to deal with a 600-foot fall instead of the usual 200 to 300.

"Where'd you drop it?" Drummond radioed.

"On the runway."

Using headlights and flashlights, the PJs watched while Phil Yezierski drove the SusV. "We'll never find this stuff," Yezierski soon thought. "It's not on the runway."

"It's on the runway," Paff said. Three seconds later, there it was.

Yezierski could drive the PJs to an elevation 800 to 1,000 feet above the crash. The slope distance was a quarter-mile or more and quite steep. Loomis and Paff slid down with medical supplies while Drummond stayed to learn what else was needed. Overhead, the Kingbird dropped 1.5-million-candlepower magnesium flares that lasted 3.5 minutes each.

First to approach the Caribou, Loomis could scarcely believe his eyes. The plane had been tossed onto the only almost flat spot on the entire mountainside. It was a terrace-like bench with a 20-degree top 30 yards wide. Anywhere else would have meant a crash into the mountainside or a rolling, jouncing, parts-scattering ride down the steep slope. Downhill wind and snow was slapping the plane broadside and howling through broken cockpit windows. The battered tail section hung over the edge of the bench, still attached by a bulged piece of fuselage floor. Winds pummeled it, shaking the whole plane and threatening to kite everything down the mountain.

Loomis knocked on the fuselage. "We're here," he said. "Anybody home?" He squeezed through the split at the tail section, illuminating the wreck with a big eight-cell scuba diving flashlight he carries on all missions. Munson was 15 feet behind the pilot's seat shivering uncontrollably. In his stage of hypothermia, Loomis thought, he had another hour at most, and if he hadn't crawled out of the cockpit and covered himself, he wouldn't have been alive to signal the rescuers. Finding Munson treatable, Loomis quickly moved to the co-pilot. "The co-pilot is deceased," he said as Paff entered the plane minutes later. "Verify that, and radio Mike that we have a survivor and will need the backboard and litter."

Of several possible injuries, one was definite. "Jim," Loomis said, "we'll have to splint your broken leg from ankle to knee. The problem is, I can't give you morphine for the pain. You're hypothermic, you have all this super-cold blood in your extremities and your body has constricted its circulation to conserve core warmth. Morphine dilutes the veins a bit, and that would cause the super-cold blood to circulate, hit the heart, and possibly cause cardiac arrest."

Munson clamped his mouth shut and braced for the worst. He did so well that, puzzled and wondering if the leg really was broken, Paff was moved to ask if it hurt.

"It hurts like hell," Munson answered and returned to silent acceptance.

Drummond arrived with the backboard and cascade litter—a shallow plastic tub with handholds. All three carefully raised Munson's 185 pounds onto the backboard, strapped him down, and slid him into sleeping bags along with chemical warming pads.

Now the question was how to get him out. The tail split was too narrow and dangerous. Jagged metal flapping in the wind could cut and disable someone. "The window on the port side is already broken out," Drummond said. "If we could cut the metal down from either side of the window, then fold that flap over, we'd have plenty of room."

Loomis, anticipating neck and back problems, installed a collar on Munson's neck while the other two searched the plane for something to cut metal. "There's a tool box by that window," Munson said. Inside were tin snips.

"I need an ax to start the cuts," Paff said, and a minute later, Munson had directed him to an ax. "Unbelievable! This guy is prepared for everything. With a little help from us, he's saving his own life."

Paff's first swing with the ax sent a shower of sparks from wires along the wall. Fuel had spilled all over, and now there was the danger of fire, if the plane didn't blow off the bench first. "Wasn't it careless not to shut off the power when you first got here?" Drummond demanded.

"Jim said he cut the power before he left the cockpit," Loomis answered. "Both of us double-checked it. It's off."

Since the main power switch in nearly all planes is between the battery's hot side and the buss feeding the wiring, jagged metal had evidently pinched a short circuit around that switch. With the wiring hot, and the insulation damaged by the crash, those wires would shower sparks when jolted enough to ground out against the metal of the fuselage. The battery access was under the plane, so no disconnect could be made there. Urgently, the PJs went on chopping and cutting, just hoping the fuel was too cold to be volatile enough to ignite.

Finally, the opening was large enough. With only his nose exposed, Munson was lashed to the litter and carried out of the dangerous aircraft. A day and a half later, the tail section was spotted a mile down the mountain.

Twenty yards from the plane, the incline rose from 20 degrees to 35; but even in the darkness between flares, the climb seemed less difficult than expected. Paff was pulling at the front, Loomis and Drummond at the sides. It was slipping, sliding, hard work, but as they paused for a breather after 20 minutes, they felt good about their progress. Just then, the HC-130 was back with another near-daylight flare. Three heads turned to check their distance from the plane, and three stomachs sickened. Twenty minutes, and they had gone nowhere.

"It doesn't matter," Drummond said. "Whatever it takes, we still have to get him up the hill. Let's go."

The second attempt was like the first, except they could see. They pulled, but the litter slid back as they tried to move forward for the next pull.

Loomis was having a well-deserved guilt trip. From the air, the snow had looked deep and benign. He had been vocal. No, he was not taking crampons. He would take snowshoes that fit on the more comfortable Ice King boots. Drummond acquiesced. Paff left his crampons behind, but wouldn't switch from hard-toed, heavy-lugged climbing boots. Surprise! What had appeared benign was really ice covered by a thin coat of crusted snow on a scree slope. The tiny ice grousers under the snowshoes gripped a bit, but spiked crampons would have been ideal.

"Why don't we change position?" Loomis suggested. "Paff, you could get behind. Kick your toes into the crust, and hold the litter from sliding when Mike and I reposition for the next pull."

Hooray! Munson was moving uphill . . . but only inches at a time. How many inches in a quarter mile? How many pulls? How much time? Often, they lost more ground than gained, and the slope would soon be steeper.

Fighting gravity and 50-mile-per-hour winds besides the ice and slick crust, Drummond and Loomis frequently slipped to their knees or butts. Gaining inches was frustrating, losing ground worse. The men commented on the conditions in loud, creative language, so much so that from inside the sleeping bag Munson voiced a muffled hope that the PJs wouldn't become so angry they'd leave him behind. Instead, they gradually learned that falling down didn't have to be their enemy if they all fell together. While a standing pull gained inches, falling up the mountain with their ropes across their hips or shoulders—if Paff also pushed from behind—advanced them several feet.

Even while they were getting up and moving forward for the next fall, the pullers couldn't leave all the weight on Paff, however. They weren't worrying Munson by discussing it, but all three were keenly aware that if everyone lost footing at once, it would send them into a mile-long slide they couldn't survive. In fact, disaster would take less than their all losing their footing at the same time. Once, when the incline had increased to 40 degrees, Loomis's feet went out from under him during a forward fall. Away he slid. Paff and Drummond were barely able to hold on to the litter when Loomis hit the end of his rope. Loud creative language was now directed at him.

Privately, each wondered what they would do if all went into a slide simultaneously. Would they hang on? Training insists they do what it takes to rescue the victim. Training also insists they not risk the team. Would they let go and fend for themselves? Each arrived at only one conclusion. They'd never again be on a mission without crampons.

Forty minutes into the arduous climb, Drummond's radio blared that the Kingbird was out of flares. In a stressed voice, the pilot explained that he could offer no further help and must return to the base. With a severely overcast sky and strong winds blowing loose snow into their faces, visibility dropped to near zero without flares. They had survival gear—food, water, tents, stoves, extra clothes—but everything was in the SusV. All had flashlights, but they couldn't hold them while pulling with both hands.

Three A.M. had passed. They were approaching twenty-four hours of physical activity, and the bleak outlook suddenly had them feeling too exhausted to go on. Although Munson had feared it, nobody yet viewed him as an albatross.

"Well," said Drummond, "We still know which way is up. Pull!"

Phil Yezierski, still at the top in his SusV, watched the Kingbird leave. The PJs sure could use my headlights, he thought, but I'd have to drive over the edge to aim them downhill. Nope, the angle is too steep. With this ice, it would be suicide.

Yezierski grabbed his two-cell flashlight with alkaline batteries, walked 150 feet to the edge, and stood there shining a beam down the slope. It wouldn't help the PJs see, but they could aim at the pinpoint of light and lose no time wandering off course.

Drummond and Loomis switched from falling forward to facing the litter, pulling, and falling backward. Their arm muscles threatened to go from strained to disabled, so they changed the pull pressure to their legs or backs. When the muscles on one side threatened to quit, they changed sides. With Paff blocking from behind, and one holding his rope securely, the other came across with his rope still taut. Stopping and swapping ate minutes that added to the hours, but they had begun this mission tired. They couldn't risk being stopped by damaged muscles or total exhaustion.

Despite minus-10 temperatures and tremendous chill from 50-knot winds, they took off their caps to dissipate the body heat their intense physical effort had generated. They wore bib overalls and Gore-Tex shell jackets with pile insulation, but the jackets were open, because perspiration collecting in pile freezes, destroying the material's insulating ability. They ate handfuls of snow to further cool themselves, being careful not to overdo it because melting the snow consumed some of their already short supply of energy.

Halfway up, the overcast cleared. Visibility mercifully improved, but now they were in a rougher part of a scree slope tilted at 40-plus degrees. Sharp talus rocks sticking out of the snow had to be maneuvered around. In places the rocks had no snow or ice covering. The men changed their routes where it was possible. Where it was impossible, they had to struggle over the rocks.

Suddenly, Munson yelled that he had to throw up. The PJs quickly loosened straps, removed his neoprene face mask, and tilted the litter so he wouldn't inhale vomit. Loomis was already concerned and watchful because Munson had been unconscious for an hour and a half in the plane. Patients with head injuries tend to throw up when placed in certain horizontal positions. All along, Loomis had been asking Munson questions to test his ability to answer rationally. Just as suddenly, Munson no longer needed to vomit, so they moved on. Claustrophobia, perhaps.

Finally, at 6 A.M., after nearly three-and-a-half hours of near superhuman struggle, they were 200 feet from the top. There they stopped cold. Inclines of over 40 degrees had been bad enough. Now the slope rose sharply at almost 60 degrees. Sleep-deprived, totally drained in muscle and mind, they stood wondering how to overcome this last, worst challenge.

"Can I help down there?" called the SusV driver, who had stood at the rim this whole time.

"I don't think so," Drummond answered, remembering that Yezierski wore warm bunny boots that aren't for climbing. And then Drummond half remembered. "Is there rope in your vehicle?"

"Yes."

"Tie it to the bumper and bring the end down."

Paff was sent back to the plane to retrieve medical kits. Drummond tied the rope to the litter with a 20-foot tag end that he and Loomis could hang on to going up. On signal, Yezierski slowly drove the SusV away from the rim, towing Munson to the top. More heating pads from the survival gear were placed around him, and minutes later an Army Air National Guard helicopter from Bethel arrived to transport him to Iliamna, from where the same Kingbird, with a different crew, flew him to Anchorage.

Jim Munson lived through the crash and escaped hypothermia, and after a lot of pain his broken arm and leg healed. What he didn't escape, and what hasn't healed, is his terrible guilt over a good friend's death—never mind that it was unforeseeable and unavoidable—while he was at the controls.

Munson sold SouthCentral Air.

# 7

*Perhaps no other couple has suffered through the worst Alaska's wilderness has ready for people who drop their guard for a moment, then returned soon after to challenge the higher elevations for another record goat.*

DAYLIGHT usually brings hope, but there was precious little of either when the long night finally ended. Roger and Pat Stewart were socked in at 3,700 feet by dark storm clouds, a dense fog that whipped sleet and heavy rains about them. Roger realized he had to get them down from the shelf they were on. They'd never last another night.

He left Pat under their makeshift shelter and set out to find a way down. Visibility was good for 25 or 30 feet, but sometimes he groped like a blind man as the fog and rain closed in. Several times, as he felt his way down chutes, Roger nearly stepped out into thin air when a chute gave way to a sheer drop without warning. He'd panic and grab a rock, clenching with all his might until he regained composure. Roger knew that if he slipped on a wet, icy rock and fell, he and Pat were both doomed.

Above all, Roger couldn't believe that with their combined experience in the wild, Pat and he were fighting for their lives. The goat hunt they were on was just one of six two-week hunts the couple had planned. At forty-five, Roger had been bowhunting big game for twenty-five years. He had taken 150 animals and had eleven species in the record books.

Pat and Roger spent their honeymoon hunting Sitka blacktail deer on Kodiak Island, and they had returned every year to celebrate their anniversary with a hunt. Twelve years before, Pat had gotten tired of merely tagging along and said, "You know, I could do that, too." For one-and-a-half years she held the world record for Sitka deer, and she had placed five other species in the Pope and Young Club record book.

The couple had always made it a point to prepare extensively before a hunt to avoid taking unnecessary chances. They always carried a three-pound tent that could withstand 50- to 60-mile-per-hour winds. They were never without a three-day supply of freeze-dried food, Roger always carried a 100-foot rope, and they bought the best in clothing and boots.

Yet, unbelievably, here they were with a space blanket for a tent. They had finished their only food by 10:30 the morning before. The rope was at base camp. Both wore wool and polar fleece, but no insulated underwear. Roger's cap had blown away in the wind. And to top it off, he had tennis shoes on his feet instead of hunting boots. As much as both emphasized safety while hunting, this time they had allowed themselves to walk, step by step, into the trap that Alaska sets for people who drop their guard, if only for a moment.

They had flown to Terror Lake, a place named for its inhospitable terrain and the unpredictable winds that buffet the region. A hydroelectric power plant had been built there about a decade ago, and the men at the plant, friends of the Stewarts' charter pilot, Jack Lechner, were aware that they had packed their provisions to Shotgun Lake, at 2,100 feet.

From the base camp at Shotgun, they had easy access to a high plateau where they could hunt goats from above their bedding areas on the surrounding cliff. They had several chances to shoot animals as close as 10 to 12 yards on the first day, but they passed on those shots because they could not scale down the steep cliffs to recover the goats.

EXTREME OUTDOOR ADVENTURES

It was their hope to catch the goats moving up to the plateau to feed. For the next two days, however, winds of up to 50 miles per hour kept them away from the cliff. Roger tried crawling to the edge to scout for goats, but without the advantage of height he couldn't see far enough over the rim. Standing was out of the question; he would have risked being kited over the brink by an unexpected gust.

The winds abated somewhat on the fourth day, and the sun shone brightly. The Stewarts hiked about three miles from camp to a place called Widgeon Bowl, where they suspected the goats might be feeding.

Around 2 P.M., Pat spotted a lone billy moving up to feed on the edge of the bowl. She quickly worked her way above his route, and five minutes after she set up an ambush, he emerged from the rocks not five yards away. The billy was too close, however, and as Pat began a slow draw, he bolted.

The rains returned the next day, but Roger was getting restless cooped up in the tent, so he set out to hunt alone. About noon, he spotted a billy bedding in a bowl 200 feet above several nannies and kids. Knowing where one of the escape routes led, Roger threw a boulder over the edge, gave a wild-man scream, and ran to intercept the goat's escape.

The goat headed directly for the ambush, and when he stepped into the open Roger let an arrow fly. It struck the billy high in the lungs. He stumbled for several yards, went over the edge, and tumbled 150 feet to the bottom of a fast-sloping shale slide.

The slide was risky, so Roger went down to the bowl and worked his way back up to the goat. Still, there was no easy route. He fell twice, and the wind whisked away his cap after the second tumble. Most troubling was the state of his feet after the arduous climb. What had started as a mild chafing on his heels had gradually worsened with each tricky foothold, until sharp pains were searing up his heels. By the time he reached the billy, the skin had been torn from the Achilles' portion of both heels.

It was cloudy and windy on September 18, the sixth day, but Pat and Roger decided to make a short excursion anyway. Pat was excited that Roger got a goat, and she wanted to scout more of the cliffs surrounding Widgeon Bowl, where the couple had seen a number of goats on their flight in.

Because it was to be a short scouting trip through easy terrain, and because both of Roger's feet were sore, he wore the tennis shoes he ordinarily used only around camp. They got an early start, and by 10 A.M. were hungry enough to stop and eat the only sandwiches they'd packed for the day. They had left the freeze-dried food, the rope, and the little tent behind at base camp. After all, they were only going to take a quick look.

Unfortunately, the cliffs Pat and Roger had seen from the aircraft were not visible from this end of the bowl. To bring the cliffs into view it would be necessary to go farther down, then traverse the incline.

Finding a passable descent was difficult, but they eventually stumbled onto a rock slide hidden by the terrain. By now the reconnaissance was taking longer than anticipated, but Roger and Pat weren't concerned. After a quick glassing of the cliffs, they would return to camp.

Without warning, at around 2 P.M. the winds picked up to 50 miles per hour, blowing in heavy storm clouds that produced a thick, whirling fog. It seemed a trap was closing in, so Roger and Pat rushed back to find the rock slide. They searched frantically, but couldn't locate the route. The slide had been well concealed even in good light. Now, in the fog and driving rain, finding the slide was pure guesswork. Every time they thought they'd found it they'd scramble up, only to run into a cliff wall. The rain turned colder and soaked them to the skin. Soon it became sleet that painfully peppered their faces. Shelter was urgently necessary, but all they had was one space blanket, held down with rocks. That night passed minute by minute, without a wink of sleep. If it hadn't been for their good health and advanced conditioning, one or both would have died of hypothermia.

Around midnight, things began to ice up. The sleet changed to hail, and they would howl in pain when a large ball of ice would find a tender target. When daylight brought no change in the storm, it was clear that they would never find the rock slide. It was now a question of getting to a lower elevation or perishing. Roger tried to descend a number of chutes, but they always ended on the open face of a cliff. Finally the wind began blowing open patches in the fog. For five or six seconds there would be a window of visibility. Through one of them Roger saw another bowl about 500 feet below.

Neither Stewart had an idea what would be around the rim of that bowl. Probably there would be more cliffs, but this was the only hope. A single tricky descent down a steep, narrow cut filled with very loose rocks was the only route down. Slowly, they picked their way.

Cliffs did indeed border the little bowl. At first there appeared to be no way off. After a better look, however, they noticed that in places the cliffs were not quite vertical. They were too steep to climb down, but they were sloped enough that alder bushes could grow here and there between the rocks.

Roger dropped over the edge and caught the first bush to stop his fall. Pat slid down and he caught her. They literally fell from bush to bush, sometimes sliding 15 or 20 feet before Roger could stop his fall. Keeping this up for another 1,000 feet, they arrived, scratched and bleeding, in the gorge below. They were now at 1,600 feet.

The cliffs shielded them from the unrelenting wind, but fog and rain perpetuated their misery. Roger's feet had become wrinkled and soft in his wet, cold tennis shoes, and new blisters were beginning to form on the bottoms of them. The hunters had been soaked for more than twenty-four hours, and a fire was absolutely imperative.

Roger had brought a lighter along, and they still had paper wrappers from their last meal stuffed in plastic lunch bags. Yet every piece of wood on the mountain was soaking wet, and the rain and sleet continued. Roger began whittling off the wet outer layers of dead sticks and cutting their dry parts into small shavings.

An hour later, he was out of paper and no closer to having a fire. He had practiced lighting emergency fires in his backyard at home, but nothing could have prepared him for the adversity of their predicament. The shavings kept burning up before anything bigger dried enough to ignite. Roger had reservations about burning the topographical map, but his hands were again shaking badly from first-stage hypothermia. He knew that if he didn't get a fire built now, he never would.

Roger committed the map to memory and burned it. Still, no fire. Finally, he thought of plastic. When it burns, it drips and keeps on burning. He lit the Ziploc lunch bags and within moments a modest fire came to life. They had been handed a new grip on life. Finally they could dry out, and then take turns sleeping while the other kept a fire watch.

The weather was still alternating between drizzle and heavy rain the following morning, but the hunger headaches and stomach growls the couple had experienced during the first two days were almost gone. They were warm and dry now, but had not been able to locate food. Both hated to move on, but they were steadily growing weaker. Logic demanded that they get to the ocean to find food and shelter, so they plodded on.

By that afternoon, their speech seemed slower. They needed to sit and rest more often.

The only route from the gorge in the direction of the ocean was down another steep slope. It was not as harrowing as the bush-to-bush drop of the day before, but it had its own price. Covering the mile and a half down to 800 feet of altitude required seven hours of painful struggle through dense, dying growth that had frosted over in the early Alaskan winter. Alder leaves and devil's club leaves as big as a man's chest were beginning to rot in the wet weather. It was a slick mess with a sting like jellyfish. If Roger and Pat slipped, they grabbed handfuls of thorny devil's club. If they stepped on a length of devil's club, a vertical section flew up at them like a rake handle full of half-inch needles. As they emerged from this jungle, every inch of their exposed skin was stuck full of needles and bleeding from scratches. Roger's feet now pained him terribly.

At the fork of two rivers, they made camp. Gulls flew past, and the air was scented with salt. They were close to reaching the ocean, but fast losing strength. Every time Roger leaned over he came up dizzy and disoriented. Collecting firewood became a difficult task. They longed for the goat meat back at camp, but that was many miles away. At least there was water. When a night's rest didn't improve their condition, they decided it would be best to conserve energy by staying put. They cleared a sandy area, built an SOS sign in 10-foot letters made of white rocks, and prayed for help.

What they didn't know was that Jack Lechner had heard about the hurricane-force winds they had encountered, learned that they hadn't sought refuge at the power plant, and began searching for them on the second day. He flew over their destroyed base camp and expected to find them somewhere on the cliffs.

On the fifth morning, Pat spotted Jack's plane about 100 feet below the fog that still covered the upper mountain reaches. She called Roger excitedly. They had rehearsed a plan. The space blanket, functioning as a lean-to, was tied down with slipknots at the corners. If a plane flew over, Pat would run to the right side and Roger to the left. Each would pull corresponding slipknots, then race into the open with the blanket to flash first the silver side, then the red.

When they had to do it for real, however, it was pure Laurel and Hardy. Roger stumbled through the fire, kicking coals in every direction. Pat beat him to the blanket, pulled her two knots, and tried to run off with the blanket before Roger had yanked a knot free. Finally, they flashed the blanket, but Jack was too far away to see it.

They had now been five days without food, and Roger began to worry about his peculiar behavior. While searching for firewood, he would lean over to pick up a piece and suddenly find himself sitting on the ground, thinking things that had nothing to do with gathering wood. The oddest part was that he couldn't remember sitting down.

They saw Jack's plane two more times that day, and then he was gone.

Around 4 P.M., they heard a popping noise in the distance and scrambled out with the space blanket to flash signals near the SOS sign. A huge red-and-white Coast Guard helicopter appeared where Jack's plane had been searching. They shouted and flashed the blanket, but it soon left, too.

An hour later the chopper returned. Again, the Stewarts flashed the blanket crazily. The chopper stopped in midair. The nose dipped toward them very slowly. "It's us!" they yelled.

The chopper eased toward them and landed beside the SOS. Pat and Roger danced as five figures clad in hunter orange jumped out, including Jack Lechner, who had been refusing charter flights until they were found.

The rescuers hadn't been searching in the right vicinity because they hadn't believed it was possible for anyone to get off those cliffs. The Stewarts also learned that the wind at Terror Lake had reached 100 miles per hour on the night they were lost, totally destroying their base camp.

They were too overjoyed at being discovered, however, to care about their equipment. They had escaped the wrath of Kodiak's mountains, and if they were hungry and weary, they were also wiser. They had made some near-fatal miscalculations when they set out on their "quick" excursion. But for all the bad decisions they had made on that unforgettable day, Roger remains convinced that conditioning, preparation, and some very good decisions saved their skins during the harrowing days that followed. Pat lost 8 pounds and Roger lost 16 during their ordeal.

Despite their five-day bout with hypothermia and starvation, neither required hospitalization.

Roger's goat was recovered and scored 46¾ Pope and Young Club points. Less than two weeks after their rescue, the pair returned to Kodiak Island, where Pat became the second woman ever to arrow a goat. It scored 47½ points.

# 8

*According to Alaska State Trooper Mike Opalka, since survivor type rescuers invented solutions to the dangers of glacial silt, no lives have been lost.*

OF ALL THE TRAPS Alaska has waiting for everyone from greenhorns to widely experienced outdoorsmen, the most insidious are the so-called mudflats. They look inviting to duck hunters, fishermen, and clammers. And once the tidewater recedes, tourists and other uninitiated innocents find mudflats ideal for taking walks—long ones, of maybe three to five miles. It's as solid as a street. Walk, run, jump up and down on it—unless you see a wet spot. Step in that, and you're in a leg-hold trap with a 500-pound grip.

While the locals know it as mud, others "educated" by the movies are inclined to call it quicksand. It isn't. And quicksand isn't what the movies lead us to believe, either. Quicksand is common sand under which is a spring or some other water that exerts pressure from below that's roughly equal to the weight of the sand. This somewhat suspends the sand. It looks like it might bear weight, but the water-lubricated sand is no more solid than the water itself. It does not suck you down, but if you stand in it, you will sink. That makes it dangerous only if you can't swim. Swimmers need only roll over and swim right out.

Alaska's trap is unique. It's made from glacial silt, rock that's been ground down over millions of years to the fineness of talcum powder or Portland cement. Like concrete, it sets hard as rock when the water drains out of it, due to its microscopic angular edges, which lock together.

Unlike concrete, the hard rock it consists of does not hold moisture for hours, like ground limestone does. When the tide drains out, glacial silt becomes as solid as rock, unless there's a low spot that doesn't entirely drain. Step in that and, lubricated by the remaining water, you slowly sink. Fight it, and you push yourself in deeper.

Roger Chasin, a thirty-three-year-old soldier from Fort Richardson, Alaska, drowned when he got caught in the glacial silt of a tidal slough. When he couldn't be freed, the barrel of his shotgun was removed for him to breathe through, until the tide covered that as well.

On opening day of duck season in 1981, Tony Chain of Anchorage found glacial silt to be "mud like glue" when his waders stuck fast. Both of his feet were mired. He tried to rock sideways, to no avail. He sank deeper with each movement until he was up to his chest in silt. Anchorage's Elmendorf Air Force Base dispatched a helicopter to the scene. Para-rescuemen harnessed Chain to the aircraft. While the chopper tilted forward, back, and sideways in tiny moves, Chain furiously scooped water and silt. Forty-five minutes later the suction broke.

Susan Winkler, a geologist with the U.S. Geological Survey who spent years studying Alaska's Cook Inlet sediments, had a frightening brush with glacial silt one sunny day during her research. Shortly after a helicopter had dropped her in the middle of Anchorage's Turnagain Arm to take water measurements, she witnessed the surface around her suddenly "liquidating." "It just waved—a whole area of 20 feet around me was liquefying," she said. The chopper was still there, and quickly lifted Winkler out of the quagmire.

In 1984, Wasilla volunteer firemen threw a rope to Tim Dortch, twenty-four, an Army man attached to Fort Richardson, and told him to tie it onto his body as low as possible. In the past Dortch had successfully survived brushes with some of Alaska's most treacherous patches of glacial silt, but today his luck changed. "My body started going down fast," he recalled. "I couldn't stop sinking. My circulation ceased from the waist down, and I continued getting lower until firemen arrived dragging high-powered hoses. They stretched the hoses over ladders they laid horizontally on the silt, to act like snowshoes that would hold their weight so they could jam hose nozzles down each side of my body." The nozzles did their work, blasting water inch by inch into the cement-like silt until it finally let go. The bruises on his body lasted a month.

In another story, Bob Huff and his wife were gazing out their picture window at ducks and geese across Cook Inlet flats when they noticed Sam Grimmet, seventeen, a young man stumbling, falling, and making no progress though seawater that had begun rushing into the tidal basin. Huff called firefighters, then went outdoors on his lawn waving a flashlight in Grimmet's direction. "I saw lights and fired my gun a couple of times, but I was stuck in a hidden trough," Grimmet said later after a paramedic and diver in an inflatable boat had rescued him.

Michael Spaulding of Fort Richardson, Alaska, was wearing heavy rubber chest-high waders to hunt ducks on the flats with two buddies. It was low tide. The air was chilly. The men separated, each going his own way. But when Spaulding felt he had gone too far out and turned to go back, his feet didn't go along. Both were gripped by glacial silt. The more he struggled, the deeper they sank. And he knew that the tide would be coming back in at a rate of an inch a minute.

Spaulding's buddies heard his call and scrambled through thickets, gathering fallen branches to throw out to him, but he could not reach them. Finally, and more sensibly, his buddies went for help.

Rather than drown, and just in case he made it, Mike held his 12-gauge shotgun high, dry, and in workable condition.

Freezing water was up to his chest when fire trucks arrived. Firemen threw ladders out to Mike, then came out and tied a rope around his body. Spaulding watched in horror as they fastened the rope's other end to the truck. He heard the engine roar. The rope tightened. "No," he screamed and waved. "I can't take it!" The rope fell limp.

NOT QUICK, NOT SAND, QUICKSAND

The firemen had another idea. One young fireman crawled to him on the ladders. Two men in back of him dragged a firehose. The young man pushed the brass nozzle of the hose toward him, yelling, "Grab it, Mike. Aim it down toward your body." Spaulding handed over his gun. He gripped the nozzle. The hose came alive, bucking, kicking, spurting warm water. Trying to hang on to it, Mike accidentally got the nozzle down inside his waders, which ballooned out and loosened the grip of the silt. He was pulled out of the waders, which remained behind.

There's a tendency among men to take chances, and of course these challenges develop the survivor personality. Still, men aren't necessarily very sympathetic when other men take chances and end up injured or worse. There's a sort of feeling that they should have known better. And some of the men who have become stuck in glacial silt did know better. They knew just how high the risks were, and went out on the flats taking chances anyway.

When a woman, especially a young and inexperienced woman, gets into trouble in the outdoors, the reaction is entirely different. We're talking about Adeana Dickison.

Jay Dickison had been living in Alaska for a time, but was from Nevada. He went back to marry Adeana and bring her to live in Eagle River, Alaska. They had been married about a month, and enjoyed placer mining for gold.

Early this July morning in 1988, Jay and eighteen-year-old Adeana rode out onto the flats in a four-wheeler towing dredging equipment in a trailer. They intended to look for gold up Seattle Creek, and the fastest way to get there from the Ingram Creek area, where they were, was across the flats. The tide was out, and the flats were quite solid.

What they didn't know was that the Ingram Creek channel out into the flats is low, and doesn't entirely drain. Wherever still water sits in glacial silt, those tiny particles that resemble volcanic ash fail to get packed solid. The Dickisons tried to cross it, and the four-wheel all-terrain vehicle promptly bogged down.

They thought they might be able to push it out, another indication of how little they knew about glacial silt. Jay was driving, so Adeana slid off and tried to push from behind. Her feet sank in, of course, and when she pushed she drove them deeper.

Jay got off and started the suction dredge to pull the silt away from Adeana's legs. He succeeded in freeing one leg before the dredge clogged or broke down and wouldn't restart. Jay kept trying to dig the other leg free, but couldn't. To compound the problem, Adeana was wearing hip boots that had a lace-up device at the knee to hold them on. She couldn't be pulled out of her boots.

Although it was still very early in the morning, at least two hours had gone by, and Jay knew they needed help. The tide was coming in. It's the second highest tide in the world, reaching 36 to 38 feet at a rate of 5 feet per hour.

Jay ran about a mile and a half before he found a parked car. The people were camping, and still asleep. They had to drive him five miles to find a phone. The call got Emergency Services rolling, but that takes time. Meanwhile, the tide kept coming in, and Adeana was stuck in one of the lower channels, which fill up quicker.

Alaska State Trooper Mike Opalka got the call at 7:52 A.M. He called the Girdwood Fire Department, then went ahead to see the situation. He walked over to the firefighters, who were just arriving, and then returned to find that the water had risen to Adeana's face. He gave her a piece of hose from the suction dredge, hoping she could breathe through it when the water climbed over her head. She was terrified, and screaming. Opalka promised that they'd get her out.

Firefighters were helping him try to pull her free. The 38-degree water was moving swiftly and Adeana was becoming hypothermic. She was now breathing through the hose. Opalka was holding her up by the armpits. Adeana weakened and lost the hose. Opalka held her as she drowned.

♦

Adeana Dickison's tragic death was the last straw. The terrible event weighed on everybody's minds. Church services honored the young woman's memory around the state.

Jim Ness, proprietor of a plumbing business outside of Anchorage, talked about Adeana to fellow members of the Alaska Mat-Su Borough Dive Rescue Team, one of whom, Bob Hancock, later phoned Ness's home anxiously. "Jim," he said with emotion in his voice, "we've got to figure out how to save those people." That evening there came together a mission that consumed the entire Dive Rescue Team's attention. "We worked on ideas," Ness said. "When I could spare time from my plumbing business, I was experimenting in the garage. Nothing seemed promising until Bob's idea of a long steel pipe jammed in the silt near the foot of the victim to break the suction."

Maybe, someone suggested, it could even be a hollow pipe with a flared perforated end through which air could be pumped.

The device was tested on the muddy coastal flats of Cook Inlet. One team member played the victim. Other members kneeled on styrofoam Boogie Boards. "It didn't quite work," Ness said. "We forced air down the pipe, and all we got were bubbles."

The men consulted with engineers throughout the long winter months, but there was no progress to report until Ness, stopping at a gas station to fill a low tire, pressed the hissing hose against an air valve. That was when he had a revelation. "The air we had pumped through the pipe, I realized, wasn't powerful enough," Ness said. "But why not blast pressurized air from a scuba diver's tank down the pipe, and use a screw-type valve to control it?"

Under carefully controlled conditions, the team experimented by putting a volunteer in silt up to his thighs. The trapped foot wouldn't budge. The air holes had clogged.

As Ness lay in bed later, staring into the darkness, the answer came to him: Drill the holes farther up the pipe.

With the bottom welded shut to keep the silt out, the team members closed the initial holes, then drilled five more in the shape of a T an inch and a half up the flared end. Short air blasts let the experimental "victim" raise his foot a few inches.

The moment of truth came on June 15. Kris Armstrong, riding his four-wheeler on a trail in the Talkeetna Mountains foothills, hit a moss-covered wet spot and lurched forward into muck he couldn't get out of. He kept sinking. His partner tossed him a rope to winch him out, but the silt held. Kris screamed, "Stop! You're tearing me apart!"

The partner went for help and returned with two men who placed a large inner tube around Kris. Fruitless pulling dislocated an ankle and tore ligaments in his knee.

Soon the partner called 911, and the Dive Rescue Team arrived with Boogie Boards and the rescue tool. Armstrong was now in up to his armpits, and pale from six hours of immersion. A squeeze on the hose valve blasted 125 pounds of air into the silt beneath him. Rescuers pulled together at Kris's arms, but he stuck fast. One more blast of air, and his right foot lifted several inches. But the silt reasserted its grip.

Then a series of blasts gave Kris enough room to move a little. More blasts, and one foot emerged. Then came the other. A life had been saved in memory of Adeana Dickison.

Since that day, inquiries about the rescue tool have flowed in from all across the United States. "We send instructions free of charge," Ness said. "Thanks have come from all over."

Just before the Adeana Dickison tragedy, and before the resulting tools to beat the glacial silt, another duck hunter with hip boots got himself up to his waist. He fired shots, and other duck hunters came to see who was yelling for help. Firemen were summoned and got ladders on both sides of him. Standing on the ladders, they got him out by physically pulling him up very, very slowly because others had leg joints damaged by pulling too fast. The silt slowly released him, but hung on to everything else—pants, boots, and underwear . . . as a television camera recorded the event.

# 9

*Dr. Siebert's theory that challenging yourself is the way to become a survivor has no more perfect proof than Donald Wyman.*

OUTDOORSMAN Donald Wyman knew all too well that sometimes the best decision is also the hardest decision. Almost everybody has heard the extraordinary story of Wyman, the thirty-seven-year-old outdoorsman who cut off his own leg. When he was alone one evening cutting down trees at his work site, he was the victim of a freak accident when a massive cut tree trunk launched itself at him like a battering ram, throwing him backwards and pinning him to the ground. Barely able to move, with his leg shattered, and with no way to get help, he was forced to make the most harrowing decision of his life.

Of course, for most of us, it's impossible to hear the horrifying details of this story without imagining—in fact, feeling—the excruciating agony Donald Wyman experienced. And as we read about this ordeal, most of us will ask some difficult questions. Faced with the same unbearable circumstances, how would we react? Could we have found some other way to free ourselves? If not, would we have had the courage, the sheer strength of character, to face hellish pain and do what Wyman did? And there are other questions: What kind of man is this guy, really? What unique traits make him the special kind of person who could do what he did? Had his many years as an avid outdoorsman uniquely prepared him for surviving this bloody, life-threatening ordeal?

To the last question, Wyman's response is immediate and unequivo-cal: "Yes, I'm sure they did." And then, thinking further, he says, "But it's such a gradual process that it's hard to say exactly how it came about."

Donald Wyman had just completed his shift as a bulldozer operator in a Pennsylvania strip mine. When a pit site widens, trees must be cleared, and Wyman had made a deal. Rather than see trees wasted, he had ac-quired permission to keep selected trees he removed on his own time.

This particular evening, Wyman chose a 26-inch oak. To avoid kick-back, he always pushed his trees over with the bulldozer instead of sawing them. When this particular oak toppled, he shoved its trunk downhill a short distance to the mine road. It would be easier to cut off the stump and root wad down there. His 16-inch chain saw wouldn't cut all of the way through, of course, so his first cut was up from underneath. Next, he sawed down from the uphill side to meet his original cut. As he did so, he felt his first cut pinching together. Mistakenly, Wyman thought the stump was trying to roll downhill. Instead, the tree was trying to spring uphill.

What Wyman hadn't noticed was that the upper part of the tree had wedged between other trees when it fell. As he pushed the trunk downhill, the oak started to flex, somewhat like a bent-sapling snare in reverse, but magnum in size and strength. With the heavy stump and root ball holding it in place, it had become nothing less than a giant trap waiting to be sprung.

"When I sawed deep enough for it to break free," Wyman says, "the spring in the tree drove the trunk at me like a Mack truck. It knocked me 10 feet, broke both bones in my lower left leg, and smashed my foot into the ground. My instant reaction was to push the tree off of me, but of course that didn't work. I was pinned. I could see that the broken bones were protruding against my pant leg about 7 inches below the knee. But the rest of my leg and foot were under the log."

Wyman yelled for help. It was unlikely that anyone would hear, but it was something to try while he cleared his head to think up other options. He had always been good at thinking up options—sometimes too good. His dad had been a steel worker and truck driver who worked a lot and couldn't always take him hunting. So Wyman's solution was to hunt alone. The game warden drove him home one afternoon, explaining why that's not an option for a boy under sixteen in Pennsylvania.

The chain saw lay 5 feet away, still running. Wyman grabbed a stick with a small branch hooking off it, pulled the saw within reach, and shut it off to conserve fuel. Exactly how to make good use of it wasn't immediately evident. The log had hit the outside of his left leg, pinning him to the ground on his right side. He couldn't twist against his trapped leg far enough to use the saw. And even if he could reach the log, the saw would cut only 16 inches deep, while the tree was 26 inches thick. Obviously, he couldn't get around to the opposite side of the log to make the second cut.

And there was another sobering thought to consider—he was probably pinned right at the tree's pressure point. Did it have any spring left in it? If someone disturbed it by cutting, would the tree butt crash into his chest or head this time?

The question was academic. Nobody was there to do the cutting anyway.

But Wyman kept yelling, though without much faith that anyone was there to hear. Janet, his wife, would not worry until after dark, when he usually came home. As she put it later, "The only thing he can't stand is being cooped up inside. He'll do anything to stay outdoors." And in his many years in the outdoors, Wyman had settled on one fundamental rule—to fill his deer tag, or switch tactics and try something else.

Now he clawed dirt out from under his leg with his bare hands. Maybe he could dig himself out.

Soon he had dug down to hardpan. A stick wouldn't loosen it. The chain saw? It worked, but three times the chain hit rocks and flew off the bar. He patiently dismantled the saw each time, careful not to lose nuts or bolts, then reassembled it. When the saw ran out of gas, he tore it down one more time and used the bar to continue digging. Finally, he could see his foot. It was totally inaccessible, smashed between the tree and bedrock.

Wyman fought the panic that threatens when your last plan of action has fallen through. All his life, he had been challenging himself—trying, testing, seeing how far he could go, what he could survive. One year he'd hiked into the Allegheny Forest with a buddy in late February to camp in minus-15-degree temperatures without a tent. On that adventure there had been no lack of ideas. They built a stone fireplace and heated the rocks all day. Spread on the ground and covered with a mat of hemlock boughs, the rocks made a warm platform for sleeping bags.

Wyman had wanted to take the challenge one step farther when small-game hunting became legal again after deer season. He proposed hiking in without food or a tent. But nobody shared his confidence that, with survival at stake, he would always be able to come up with that one great idea that would save him.

Now, however, with tons of pressure bearing down on his shattered leg, Wyman had no backup plan, no great idea. He prayed. He thought of his family. He looked around the woods and thought hard, searching for solutions. In the forest, he thought, dead limbs—and even whole trees—fall every day. So what would, say, a raccoon do if its foot got trapped under a deadfall?

He knew the answer: When the foot numbed, the raccoon would amputate it with its teeth.

Wyman had been pinned for an hour. It would be another four or five hours before his wife would suspect something was wrong. More time would pass before someone came looking. He feared he'd go into shock by that time—and people die from shock.

That was when it came to him. It was the only answer: "I could leave my leg here and live."

Wyman reached for his pocketknife. It had a narrow 3-inch clip blade. He used it for cleaning grease fittings on his bulldozer, not for skinning. He tried to slit his pant leg to see what sort of damage he had suffered. The knife wouldn't even cut cloth.

Fishing about in the dirt, Wyman found a piece of sandstone. He began to whet an edge on the blade, just as he'd done on deer hunts so often before. A lifetime in the outdoors had taught him that those who give up easily don't succeed. Now Wyman's steely determination to succeed would be put to the sternest test it would ever face.

With the roughly honed blade, he slit his pant leg.

"When I saw how bad it was, with bones sticking out and my foot smashed, I knew what I had to do," Wyman said. "I pulled the starting cord out of my chain saw for a tourniquet. Of course, a tourniquet causes damage when it's on too long. I tied it right above where it was really bad so I'd lose as little leg as possible. Then I cut my skin, sort of scratched it with the knife, to see if there was any feeling. It didn't hurt too bad. So I tried it again a little deeper. That hurt! I doubted I could do it.

"Finally, I decided there was no other way to stay alive. I got myself in a determined state of mind, grabbed my leg with my left hand, resolved not to pull back, and started cutting where the bones were already broken. It hurt terribly every time I hit a nerve or vein. My muscles jumped like frog legs in a frying pan. But I kept cutting across the top. And then I cut up from underneath until the knife came through and I could pull away.

"Blood was spurting from arteries, so I laid the chain-saw wrench across the tourniquet knot, tied another knot over it, and twisted until the spurting stopped. I gave my leg one last look and crawled 140 feet up the hill to my bulldozer."

It's never easy to climb onto a bulldozer. And since he was holding the tourniquet tight with his left hand, Wyman had only his right hand and right foot with which to climb. After two or three futile attempts, he slid onto one of the force arms holding the blade. That enabled him to crawl up the front of the track and drag himself back to the cab. Wyman started the engine and threw the automatic transmission into gear. "I was relieved to be on a piece of machinery that could take me someplace," he said. "My truck was a quarter of a mile away."

The pickup's four-speed standard shift posed a whole new problem. Wyman grabbed a file to extend his reach. With it, he pushed the clutch pedal, getting the transmission into first gear and leaving it there to drive.

The first two homes he came to along the road looked deserted, but a girl was playing in the third yard. "Get your dad," Wyman yelled. "I'm bleeding to death."

John Huber came out of his dairy barn cautiously—he thought this fellow was yelling like a madman. Finally, to make himself clear, Wyman raised the stump of his leg. It looked as if it had been blown off by a shotgun. Huber ran inside to call an ambulance.

"What direction are they coming from?" Wyman asked when Huber returned.

"I don't know."

"Go back and ask the dispatcher," Wyman urged. "It's faster if we meet them halfway."

Huber came back, now with a clear plan. He slid behind the controls, and they raced off. Incredibly, Wyman asked Huber to slow down so they wouldn't die in a wreck.

At the crossroads, Wyman's clear-headed thinking and planning continued. Volunteer firefighters, a rescue team, beat the ambulance to the scene. Wyman calmly drew them a map of where his leg could be located. He climbed onto the wheeled stretcher but refused a sedative, not wanting to be unconscious in case someone else got excited and made a mistake.

"I did let them give me morphine at the hospital," Wyman said later. "They had to wash the leg and clamp the arteries. Boy, that hurt! Soon after, they took me to the operating room and did a nicer job than I had. My leg followed me to the hospital by a half hour, but the doctors said it was too late, they couldn't reattach it. In fact, they said it was probably best that I had cut it off. With all the broken bones in the leg and smashed foot, I would have been hospitalized from six months to two years. It would have taken many operations to reconstruct the bones. Even then, I may never have walked as well as I do now."

Motivated by Wyman's courage, the Advanced Prosthetic and Limb Bank Foundation decided he should be one of 100 amputees to test a new technology called "Sense-of-Feel." Sabolich Prosthetics and Research Center, in Oklahoma City, fitted Wyman with a leg that has sensors on the bottom of the foot. These devices send signals to his leg muscles, which are still operating his foot, even though it isn't there. "I know when a rock is under my foot," Wyman says. "So I can avoid sliding. And it greatly helps my balance to know when the foot touches ground."

Just three months after the accident, on Sunday, October 24, Wyman had been back to work on his bulldozer for a full week. By then, he'd astounded nearly everybody in America—except those who knew him before the accident. His wife, Janet; his son, Brian; his boss, David Osikowicz; and his close friends were all aware of his strength of character. None were surprised that he was able to adjust his thinking to do whatever it took to survive.

A day earlier, the Wyman family had returned to the accident scene for the first time to sit on the log, the only remaining evidence of Wyman's horror. Somehow, Janet Wyman had expected the site to be twisted and torn—as tormented as the feelings she had about the torture her husband had survived. Instead, she found only peace and quiet. Rain had erased the bloody trail Wyman had left from log to bulldozer. The single sound was a grouse in the distance.

Don Wyman listened in silence as his wife tried unsuccessfully to reconcile the serenity she saw around them with the sorrow she felt.

She'd narrowly escaped the long suffering of widowhood. But traumatic as it had been, when all else failed Wyman had made this one heart-rending, lifesaving decision.

And now, like nature itself, he was ready to move on. "I don't mourn the loss of my leg," he says. "I'm alive and already getting around pretty well. I'm happy the way things turned out."

By December, Wyman and his son Brian were once again hunting in the Alleghenies. To no one's surprise, Wyman got his deer.

# 10

*Steve Matthes was exactly the sort of man who lives as a participant in the natural world—in contrast to the armchair spectator, so common in today's world, who knows only enough to cheer or boo.*

MATTHES was a full-time professional lion hunter for the California Department of Fish and Game when Brave was born to his bitch, Belle. In a litter with eleven red pups, Brave had peculiar dun hair that was somewhere between rough and smooth. Because he knew that no "bad blood" could have gotten into the line, Matthes picked up the pup, thinking it would have to be destroyed. At the last moment, however, he was diverted by Belle's pleading eyes.

That evening Matthes was called to eliminate a sheep-killing lion 500 miles away, on the eastern slope of the Sierra Nevada. When he returned several weeks later, the odd pup had grown odder still. He was all legs and eyes. One ear lay like a hound's, while the other tried to stand up. Matthes's wife, Vera, and son, Eddie, had become fascinated with the "funny little dog," as they called him, but Matthes didn't share their enthusiasm.

Early the next morning, Matthes walked to the kennel for one last look before culling the misfit pup. The alert "funny pup" boiled out of the box to greet him with luminous, penetrating dark eyes that seemed to convey almost human intelligence. Suddenly, from that small throat, came the loudest bawl Matthes had ever heard from a pup. In disbelief, he made a quick step toward the pup, trying to evoke another response.

Instead of jumping back and barking like a normal pup, this strange little fellow held his ground, bristled a bit, and bellowed again.

Matthes opened the gate. The whole litter, led by the precocious pup, raced 100 yards to the cage housing Matthes's pet mountain lion, Cleo. In seconds the pup located Cleo on her ledge and began baying. When the other pups joined in halfheartedly, Cleo charged the tiny pack. All of the pups, save the peculiar one, scattered like quail. The odd pup held his ground, tail between his legs and hair bristling, trying to bite Cleo through the wire. Angered, Cleo tried to bite back, caught her teeth in the mesh, and was bitten in the nose by the young hound. Matthes broke up the fight and carried the pup back to the kennel, with his opinions and intentions completely reversed.

Matthes had started in hounds with a bitch that traced its lineage back to Ben Lilly's lion and bear pack. To her genes—and her descendants'—he had added the blood of hounds from the famous lion packs of Carl Hurt, Jay Bruce, Wiley Carroll, Jack Butler, the Lee brothers, Smokie Emmett, and Gus Landergen. He had bred only lion dogs to lion dogs. In the mid-1940s, he'd intensified his line with an inbreeding program designed to produce natural lion hounds—hounds with an affinity for lions, the kind of affinity that bird dogs have for birds and beagles for rabbits.

In this weird little pup, it appeared that Matthes had accomplished that aim. He left the kennel wondering about what to name the young dog. Nothing seemed to fit.

At breakfast, Eddie wondered aloud how to name something that looked like this pup. Vera, picking up the dishes, said, "Well, the funny little thing sure is brave."

"That's it," Eddie exclaimed. "That's his name—Brave!"

At five-and-a-half months, Brave was part of the pack on a three-day lion chase. The older hounds' pads were cut and worn by shale, so Matthes called a halt, welcoming a rest himself. Instead, he was jerked awake by Brave's almost hysterical bawling at something in the dark. Throughout the night, Brave would quiet briefly, only to resume baying.

Exhausted from lack of sleep, but curious, Matthes untied Brave and his sire, Red, soon after dawn. It was a lion that Brave had smelled down in the gorge. The pair of dogs treed the cat out of hearing behind a ridge. Two hours later, Matthes found them and shot the lion. When the skinning was finished, Matthes ordered the dogs to come along, and started for camp. Brave struggled to his feet and collapsed, leaving Matthes to carry a lion hide and a 25-pound hound through thick brush and 110-degree heat.

Brave went on to enjoy a long career as Matthes's all-time best lion dog. When other hounds' feet would give out after several days on a lion that they couldn't jump or tree, Brave would have two or three days of running left. He could move a two-day-old track as if it were eight hours old. His early mad courage later became tempered with caution. Speed and alertness made him outstanding on lions that wouldn't tree. He'd dart in, bite, and leave an empty hole in the air before the lion could spin around. Brave was indeed a natural lion dog.

I was anxious to see the descendants of this brave hound. It was 1990. We couldn't chase California's protected lions, but Matthes, now well into his seventies, had invited me along on a bear hunt. Mostly, however, I wanted to meet the man. I had read the book he wrote, also called *Brave,* and the more I'd read, the more fascinated I'd become.

Matthes had wonderfully exciting stories to write, but they weren't just tales. Matthes is an extremely intelligent houndsman of deep feeling, courage, and perception. He learns from his experiences.

While trailing a cat into what he calls Medicine Flat, for example, Matthes began to notice an unusual number of old scats. They all contained great amounts of the wire grass prevalent in the area. Also prevalent in those scats were large numbers of dead tapeworms.

Matthes had plenty of time to watch as his hounds cold-trailed through the low valley—a strange place for a cat to go. Lions love high, rocky places. Sure enough, Matthes found fresh scats from the lion his hounds were chasing. These scats, too, contained wiregrass and tapeworms. After the lion was jumped, treed, and dispatched, Matthes made a careful examination of its intestines. Only a few short tapeworm segments remained attached to them. This explained why, while every lion he'd killed had carried several tapeworms, none had suffered the great infestations noticed in domestic cats. The lions knew how to cure themselves. Our dogs may eat grass for similar reasons.

I tried to catch Matthes on my way to Oregon. He wasn't home. On my way back, he was in San Bernardino. A month later I caught up with him in Arizona. California had gotten too crowded for his brother Jack, so Jack had bought a place near Camp Verde. Steve was there to help him unpack.

My wife and I arrived just ahead of the movers, who dumped everything on the ground and left. Matthes has one leg that's shorter than the other—plus constant pain—due to a wreck involving a dog, a horse, and a bear. He says that it makes the hills steeper. On that day, though, he grabbed one end of a piece of furniture, so I grabbed the other. With all of us working, we hauled everything inside before the predicted rain. And thus began the interview with a lion, jaguar, and bear hunter who has spent a lifetime being hard to catch in any one spot.

We didn't get to hunt, and I didn't get to meet Matthes's three remaining hounds. But for three days my recorder and I were privy to the experiences of a man who has truly enjoyed life, who is clever and clear-minded enough to have been anything he desired, but who chose an adventurous life above monetary wealth. The older we grow, the more we realize that success is in our life experiences, not in the numbers in a ledger. And nothing focuses us so clearly on what's genuine than a confrontation that threatens to steal from us what really counts.

◆

This happened to Matthes in the rugged California coastal range between Santa Barbara and Ventura, when Brave and the rest of his pack were cold-trailing the biggest lion of Matthes's career. As he was fighting his way through the thick, semitropical brush, he suddenly heard Brave break over the main ridge, hot behind the jumped cat. Matthes stopped. The chase was coming straight down the ridge toward him.

Matthes heard feet rustle in the leaves, and the gigantic lion came into view. It stopped in a small, 20-foot clearing, breathing too heavily to go on. There wasn't a tree tall enough to climb within a half mile, and Matthes was struck with fear. If he didn't get that lion first, it could easily kill his entire pack.

Matthes arrived at one side of the clearing at the moment Brave got to the other. He squeezed the trigger just as the lion sprang. It was a miss. But the cat turned toward the blast in midair, and Brave was able to duck into the brush.

Before Matthes could shoot again, Brave attacked from behind. The lion whirled, the rest of the pack boiled in, and there was no chance to shoot without hitting a dog. The cat came down on Red with both front feet, and bit him through the shoulder. Brave flew in and grabbed the lion by the back of its neck. The cat reached back, sank the 4-inch claws of one paw into Brave's head, and jerked him loose.

Matthes, now in the middle of the fracas, shoved the rifle barrel into the giant's mouth and fired. The cat fell. Brave was free, but it looked as if half of his head was gone.

In a wink, the lion was on its feet, only wounded in the lower jaw. Its blazing green eyes locked with Matthes's. Trying to shoot again, Matthes was knocked off his feet by a dog. He threw himself backward as he fell, somersaulted, and stopped with his back against a bush 10 feet downhill from the lion. The rifle lay between them. Paralyzed by fear, Matthes watched the cat stumble toward him, dragging dogs as it came.

At that moment the wounded Brave charged the giant head-on. Dog and lion went down with their jaws locked, and Matthes knew his dog was being killed. His fear for himself vanished. He jumped to his feet, grabbed the gun, and slammed the barrel across the lion's head. The cat didn't seem to notice, much less let go. Only a brain shot would end this struggle before Brave died, but a bullet could deflect into the dog. There was no choice. Matthes held the muzzle of the gun to the cat's head and pulled the trigger.

The lion dropped on top of Brave. Neither moved. Matthes grabbed one of the huge forelegs and rolled the cat off his dog. Brave staggered to his feet, still clinging to the huge animal's lower jaw. The courageous hound slowly released his hold and stood, proud and defiant, beside the lion. But Brave's life's blood was streaming from his terribly torn head, and Matthes was helpless to stop it. Brave lived for a short time, but no longer could hunt.

Brave was the dog who had traded his life for his master's.

# 11

*The unstoppable Susan Butcher lived for challenges, and would not quit. Why did a bad snowstorm turn her, and not the other competitors, around in her last Iditarod Race? So she could experience a new adventure!*

SUSAN BUTCHER, America's best-known adventuress and the most daring of dedicated dog people, called her sled team to a quick halt in the black of night about 150 miles outside Anchorage. A cow moose stood blocking the trail ahead.

"This has happened before," Butcher thought, optimistically. "We'll deal with it."

On another occasion, a moose, thinking it was cornered, had run through her team as it tried to escape. This time, however, Butcher's headlamp had caught sight of the huge animal when there was still plenty of distance between them. There was ample space for the moose to escape in nearly any direction it chose.

Butcher was eager to move on, of course. This was the 1985 Iditarod Sled Dog Race from Anchorage to Nome, and she was mushing the best team she'd assembled yet over seven years of learning, breeding, and training. Butcher had already set a new time record for the first leg of the trip between Anchorage and Eagle River, and her chances of winning had never been better. But an Alaska moose can be highly dangerous. Butcher would give the cow all of the time she needed to move. And move she did! The crazy cow turned and charged straight into the dog team.

Butcher reached for the .44-caliber handgun she usually kept in the sled, then remembered she hadn't packed it. "The seat belt is never buckled when you need it," she thought as she looked for an alternative. There was only the ax. Without hesitation the little woman grabbed the ax and, in her words, "went after the moose." Incredibly, she succeeded in driving the animal away from her team, but not before some of her dogs had been severely injured.

Instead of leaving, however, the moose charged back into the team, slashing with her hoofs and stomping the harnessed dogs, which couldn't get out of her way. Again, Butcher waded into the fracas swinging her ax. It wasn't just that this was a valuable team and her best chance of winning the race: these were her closest friends. Bitter childhood experience had taught her a lesson she had never managed to shake, that constant and unconditional love came only from her dogs, not people. And now her closest friends were being killed by a moose. Two were already dead.

Butcher swung with a fury. Oddly, even as Butcher fought for her dogs' lives, she was also feeling sympathy for the moose. "My God, she's so skinny! She must be starving to death!" Indeed, six cows had just starved to death in that vicinity. It was a bad winter for moose, and very likely it was starvation that made this cow behave as she did. She may have perceived this dog team to be a pack of wolves. Her instincts may have told her that she was too weak to escape by running. Her only choice if she wanted to survive would be to drive off the "wolves," which of course were harnessed together and couldn't run away.

After 20 minutes of fighting to keep the moose out of her dogs, Butcher noticed the flash of a headlamp coming up from behind her. "Moose!" she yelled long before her fellow musher got close enough to be in danger. "Tie your team. Do you have a gun?"

"Yeah!" The other musher tied his team to a tree and ran up to shoot the moose. But it was too late to salvage the team for this race.

Besides two dead dogs, thirteen more were injured. Butcher spent the next week in a veterinary clinic, helping nurse her dogs back to health.

That incident tells you the basics about Susan Butcher. An up-front woman, she's as tough as a dog harness, and honest about it. She's not trying to hide anything behind a feminine façade. Growing up, Butcher didn't think she was as pretty as she wanted to be. She figured she'd have to become strong to make up for that, and do things differently than most girls did them. In addition, she was dyslexic. Printed words transposed themselves on the page. When she read the word "dog," her brain might register it as "god." Imagine trying to understand a printed page under those circumstances! Teachers would sternly lecture her about mental laziness, usually in front of the class. After all, Butcher excelled at math. Didn't that prove that she was smart enough to learn if she would just apply herself? Back then, kids saw dyslexics as simply dumb.

To compound the girl's problems, her parents divorced. Children often blame themselves when their parents split, thinking that the marriage wouldn't have broken up if they themselves had been "better." Given her parents' divorce and her own dyslexia and doubts about her appearance, it's small wonder that the school-aged Butcher was looking for more from life. She found it with the neighborhood dogs, which she played with more than she played with other children.

Butcher was a big-time, full-time tomboy. In high school, she found that she was a natural at sports. She proved her worth over and over again in basketball, softball, and field hockey. She was fond of swimming and sailing. Sailing was special. She thrilled at taking risks in seas that kept the boys on the beach.

Given all that, in addition to a hatred for the city and a lifelong love for, and a desire to live in, the wilderness, it wasn't surprising that Butcher would become an Alaska musher. The first step in that direction came when Butcher was fifteen, and was given her first husky. The following year Butcher bought a second husky, but her mother said that the house wasn't big enough for two dogs. Rather than give up her dog, the strong-willed sixteen-year-old moved out to obtain more freedom from wilderness life in Maine.

She finished high school, then went to Fort Collins, Colorado, where she joined her father and studied at Colorado State University to become a veterinary technician. Upon arrival, she found that her stepmother had bought her a sled dog. They drove out to pick it up from a woman who owned fifty huskies. Ten minutes later Butcher had cut a deal to move in with the woman and help with the dogs' care and training.

After two years of study, work, and mushing, Butcher was still looking for more from life. She chafed under the pressure of having too many people around. She despised the people of Colorado's dropout culture, who she felt were too irresponsible to send their children to school. One of her two dogs had been stolen. The other was killed by a car. Butcher headed north, looking for a less populated place, a place where dogs and people were still partners in a self-sufficient way of life. It was 1975.

After her first month in Alaska, Butcher acquired three littermate huskies. She earned some money on a musk ox ranch and in the salmon industry. By 1977, she had moved into a gold-rush blacksmith's log cabin in Eureka. There was no running water, no electricity, no bathtub, and no people around, other than a half-dozen widely scattered seasonal miners sifting creek sand for specks of gold.

By 1978, Butcher was ready to run the Iditarod. She had a ragtag team consisting of the three littermates plus two other dogs, and she had no money to buy more. She filled out the team with whatever dogs she could find or borrow.

One of the dogs weighed 30 pounds and another 90, so the team was unbalanced. But Joe Redington, Sr., who started the Iditarod, was impressed with the race that Butcher ran with it. He couldn't quite identify it, but there was something about this young woman and the way her dogs responded to her that was quite different.

If Butcher doesn't hide behind a feminine façade, neither does she disguise her femininity.

Encouraged by Redington, she continued training in her own way. And that includes very patient caring and nurturing. Nevertheless, the dogs also recognize Butcher's strong dominance. The combination made Butcher a pack leader dogs are willing to work their hearts out for. Even that didn't serve to make her the great racer that she is, however. She's also got that extra spark: an adventurer's attitude.

In 1984, with 888 miles of the 1,157-mile Iditarod behind her, Butcher pulled into the coastal village rest stop of Unalakleet, only to learn that the overland route was closed. Most of the snow had blown away. Mushing across 40 miles of Norton Sound sea ice, mostly at night, would raise the risks considerably. But Butcher's attitude toward risk was the next thing to total blindness. That she was jockeying for the lead with two other racers was vastly more important.

Everything went well for 30 miles until Butcher neared the cliffs she had been told to avoid. Now it became necessary to double back and go around. Meanwhile, the water under the ice was turbulent, maybe on account of the huge rocks that jutted out of the sea there. Suddenly, Butcher could feel the roller-coaster sensation of ice undulating beneath her feet.

Instinctively, she called "Haw" to her lead dog, Granite. He obediently turned left toward shore, but the ice billowed upward, then fell apart as it dropped back down, dumping dogs, sled, and Butcher into 30 feet of water so cold it could kill within minutes. Granite struggled to reach solid ice, then dug his claws into the slick surface to pull himself and his bracemate out of the water. Two by two the rest of the team followed until they'd pulled the sled and Butcher from the sea.

Unwilling to trust the ice again, Butcher guided her team onto the beach. She would slowly but surely maneuver her team through the clutter of rocks and driftwood and cover the last 10 miles to Shaktoolik.

Butcher's dogs could survive the minus-15-degree temperatures with ease. Their coats were water-resistant. Butcher, however, was soaked to the skin. Hypothermia was a serious threat. But she handled it with her typical optimism, running behind the sled to warm herself and thinking, "This isn't too terrible. If it was minus 30 degrees or worse, I'd have to do something different."

Just after Butcher won the Iditarod for the fourth time, she was near St. Louis, filming promotional material for her sponsor, Purina Pro Plan. It was clear from the way she was bristling as she left the studio that, for her, filming a commercial is a worse ordeal than facing the Arctic. Later, over pizza with her husband David Monson, a champion musher in his own right, and with Granite curled up on the floor, Butcher mentally traveled back to Alaska. As she told David about some of her brushes with death, her eyes lit up and the big, winning smile we've seen on television spread across her face. Like any genuine adventurer, Butcher thoroughly enjoyed those wins against incredible odds.

Living a self-sufficient and adventurous outdoor life has its price, of course. Fortunately the costs have been lower since Monson, a lawyer, started helping her carry water, secure food and fuel, fix the generator, feed the dogs, and do all the other chores living a life of relative freedom in the wilderness makes necessary. Butcher accepts losing the tips of her toes and pieces of facial skin to frostbite as part of the dues she has to pay. There's no hospital around to fix things if she makes a mistake.

"It is an adventurous life," Monson said. "And life should be an adventure. But you learn to avoid behavior that ends in problems or pain. You're more careful in the wilderness because, though adventure is thrilling, you don't want a life-threatening experience every day."

Susan's extreme adventures didn't all happen during the Iditarod. One night, Butcher was late coming in from a training run. Dave spent an hour out looking for her, but she had taken a different route this time. Her sled hit a patch of glare ice, and she felt it going out of control. In an instant, momentum hurtled it, her, and half of the dog team off the trail and onto the steep slope of a cliff-like precipice. The dogs were howling their fright, and those still on the trail were clawing at the level ground to keep from being pulled over the edge.

Butcher climbed up to survey the situation, finding saplings blocking the way between the sled and the top of the precipice. There was no way the dogs could pull the sled through or over them. A true survivor, Susan never felt defeated; she would find a way. What she did find was a rusty old screwdriver, which repeatedly fell apart as she hacked at the trees and brush. For four hours, Susan bent the trunks over as far as possible, chopping at them with the dull screwdriver until she could break them over and twist them off. Finally, the huskies were able to pull the sled over the little stumps and up to the top, where they were safe.

Joe Redington, who started the 1,152-mile Iditarod race in honor of the old time mushers who ran this route to take serum to dying people in Nome, predicted that Susan would one day win it. She tried it for the first time in 1978, and despite her terribly unbalanced team of dogs, she won $600 for her nineteenth-place finish. She spent the money to buy Granite. The next year, Granite helped her come in ninth. In 1980 and 1981, she finished fifth. In 1982, her fifteen-dog team slid off the trail into a tree. Three dogs were injured. A snowstorm followed, and she strayed 10 miles off course in a whiteout. The injured dogs were dropped off at a checkpoint, and later she dropped off two more. Now, with just nine dogs, she raced on against winds as high as 80 miles per hour. Amazingly, she finished just 3 minutes and 43 seconds behind the winner, Rick Swenson.

Butcher finished ninth in 1983. (One of her ninth-places finishes was the result of somebody moving the signposts; otherwise she might have finished higher.) Susan was back to second in 1984. The moose ended her 1985 race.

By 1986, Butcher was back in top form. She was first to cross the finish line for a $50,000 prize. She repeated her performance in 1987 and 1988 for a record three consecutive wins. She won the last race despite suffering a wreck in muddy conditions and spending twenty-four hours repairing her sled with duct tape and a pocketknife. In 1989, she was back in second place. But she broke a course record (16 days, 1 hour, and 53 minutes) for her 1990 first-place finish, and was now tied with Rick Swenson's four wins.

In 1994 Butcher was in the lead when she ran into a dangerously violent snowstorm. She simply turned around and went back. Why was this storm more threatening to her than to the others? What could possibly stop this seemingly unstoppable competitor? After all, this was the woman who had once said, "I don't know the word 'quit.' Either I never did, or I've abolished it." There could be only one answer, and it came soon enough. Susan had her first baby girl, then had a second. She retired from racing to raise a family.

By age fifty-one, she was ill. David Munson would confidently say, "Leukemia has not yet met Susan Butcher." Despite his brave hopes, it was not a race she could win.

# 12

*Captain Thorne Tasker's instant focus and incredible strength, which were required to save his crew, were products of the "exact clarity" he had experienced twice under extreme emergency conditions. "The mind is a powerful thing," he says. "People underestimate it."*

SOME YEARS, crabs are many and worth little; other years they're few and valuable. This was an ideal year. Prices were up and crabs were plentiful. His tanks weren't filled, but Captain Thorne Tasker had $100,000 worth of crabs aboard from seventy-two hours of around-the-clock crabbing, and he wanted them safely in port at King Cove, 100 miles away.

Winds were already at 50 knots and gusting to 60. The waves had reached 25 to 30 feet. The weather station promised worse: winds up to 80 knots and 40-foot seas were predicted to hit at around midnight. Tasker ran the boat until 8:30 P.M., then told the crewman taking the watch he was going to get some rest. "Wake me at midnight. I want to be at the wheel when the worst of it gets here."

Alaska's most dangerous fishery is the winter Opilio tanner crab season in the Bering Sea, and January is the most treacherous month.

The storm had changed little by midnight, so Tasker asked the crewman, who was about to do the next two hours on watch, to wake him again at 2 A.M.

Awakened two hours later and about to take over, Tasker immediately recognized that something very serious had happened between midnight and 2 A.M. He could hear things banging around. The bookcase lurched from the bulkhead, and books scattered. The computer ripped off the wheelhouse, so now there was no navigation. The 135-foot *Norwitna* was listing 15 degrees to port. The bow was low in the water, and seas were breaking over the port rail. It seemed there was a danger of sinking.

Tasker felt certain that the problem, whatever it was, was structural, but before he discovered exactly what it was, he couldn't take chances with how serious it might be. Embarrassing as it was—he had never had to do it before—Tasker got on the radio and issued a sort of Mayday by giving the vessel's name and position and repeating it until someone repeated it back.

"I have to go down and check the engines," he told the other boat, "and I don't know the severity of the problem. Give me 10 minutes. There are six people on board."

In fishing language, that meant that if the other boat didn't hear back, it should start looking for six people in the water.

"Roger," said the other boat, and Tasker went below to tell everybody to get up and bring their survival suits with them. He told the engineer to swing the crane from the port side back across the deck to shift some weight to starboard to help balance the boat. Tasker took one crewman along to the wheelhouse to stand by on the radio, and told the others to get out on deck and discover the damage. He radioed the other boat that he was back and discussed the conditions a bit. Two other boats reported their positions.

Tasker went down to the engine room, found no water there, and decided to further shift weight by pumping fuel out of the full port "day tank" and filling an empty tank on the starboard side of the engine room. He started the pump and went back on deck to find that the crew had discovered the cover of a forward hatch missing. It had apparently been pounded off by the breaking seas and washed overboard. Waves sloshing into the hatch accounted for the bow riding low in the water.

What Tasker couldn't know was that a gooseneck vent had been sheared off on the port side. A deck plank torn free by the violent waves could have knocked it off, as could have the hatch cover on its way overboard. That gooseneck had vented the port tank. Now it was gone, and the seas washing over the port side were filling that tank with saltwater. The crew reported the broken hatch, but nobody had yet noticed that the vent was missing.

After 20 minutes of seawater pumping into the clean fuel system, both engines and the electrical generator shut down in sequence, depending on how far each was from the now contaminated starboard tank.

Tasker went below and desperately tried to find a configuration that would allow clean fuel to flow from the main tanks to the engine. Fuel arrangements are fairly standard on crabbing boats. The main tanks are located in the bottom of the boat for ballast and stability. Fuel is electrically pumped from there through filters and a centrifuge, which separates water from fuel by centrifugal force, to day tanks located high in the engine room. Fuel from the day tanks is fed by gravity to the engines. For a moment, the engines got enough clean fuel to restart, but again choked on seawater. Without the generator, there was no pump to move the clean fuel.

About 4 A.M. Tasker told the crewman who had been on watch, but who hadn't noticed that the *Nowitna* was sinking, to go down and get the men into their survival suits and stand by behind the wheelhouse. The crewman didn't panic, but his face was white. He still wasn't aware, or didn't want to believe, that they were going down. Three times he asked, "Is this just a drill?"

The Coast Guard had received the Mayday, but their nearest cutter, the *Mellon*, was 100 miles away, and that ship's helicopter could not launch into the storm. An HH-60 Jayhawk could and did take off from St. Paul Island, 155 miles away, at 5:30 A.M.

Meanwhile, in the dark with a flashlight in his mouth, Tasker was back in the engine room, still trying to work out a way to get clean fuel to the engines. As Suzanne, then his wife of seventeen years, had said, "Thorne Tasker just won't give up."

The Coast Guard had a different opinion about the captain in the engine room, and a crewman delivered their radioed message: "You gotta get out of the engine room."

"I don't think so."

"They ordered me to tell you to leave the engine room."

"Hey, I'm the skipper. You go back up to the wheelhouse."

Tasker figured the order was on a cutter commander's checklist of things to do, probably because owner/operators, in particular, can go down trying to save their boat.

While he wasn't the owner, Tasker knew the boat would be lost once he left the engine room. He persisted until the Jayhawk arrived at 8:30 A.M.

He did think of ways the fuel could theoretically move from the bottom tanks up to a high tank that could gravity-feed the engines, but moving it in practice required the now dead generator. He emerged on deck, like the crew, wearing his loose-fitting "Gumby" suit made of heavy neoprene and designed for survival in 38-degree water. All suits had retro-reflective tape on them, plus a blinking strobe light.

Except for the light shining from the bottom of the helicopter, the Alaska sky was still pitch-black on this January 22 morning. The gale-force winds and the waves of 30 feet and higher were broadside to the *Nowitna*'s starboard, pushing the crabber sideways at about 5 knots. Now and again a rogue wave, a huge wave with no obvious rhythm, would come through, causing the boat to rise and fall perhaps 40 feet. Combined with the wind, each rising wave rolled the *Nowitna* violently onto its port rail. Sliding down the backside of the wave caused a somewhat less dramatic roll to the starboard. The boat's up-and-down and rolling motions were so extreme that accomplishing the simplest tasks became almost impossible.

Upon arriving, chopper pilot Lieutenant Commander Paul Ratte took one look at what was going on below and become convinced that hoisting just one man off the *Nowitna* would be difficult. Six would be impossible. The hoist cable is 3/8 inch's worth of separated steel rated at 600 pounds. The cable is designed so that if it gets caught somewhere on the boat, and drops into a trough between waves, it will snap instead of trying to pull the chopper out of the air or yanking the winch loose. If the cable rakes across an obstruction on the ship, the little braids fray and then jam up in the winch. Lose the cable, and you're out of business.

Ratte radioed Tasker, told him the problem, and suggested that either they fly to Cold Bay, refuel, and come back by daylight, or put the men in the water away from the boat. "We have a swimmer to help them into the basket."

"I can't let my men get scattered in the water in the dark," Tasker answered very calmly. "You might have a mechanical failure or run too low on fuel before you find all of them."

Tasker sounded so calm and confident that Ratte assumed he had the crisis under control. The two agreed that coming back on a tailwind at daybreak would make the safest rescue.

Actually, Tasker did believe that having his men in the water before daylight would be a bigger risk than trying to ride it out. But that wasn't the whole situation. The fact was, his men had been just outside the wheelhouse door, listening. One had become very panicky. Tasker had to hold his men together during the wait. A good captain knows that even if order and stability don't exist, if he presents a face of order and stability, the men will relax and stay calm.

What Ratte was seeing below him and what he was hearing didn't exactly match, but the captain seemed to be in control. Ratte radioed back, "We don't have enough fuel to stay until daylight, so we'll run to Cold Bay and get back to do the hoist at daybreak."

About five minutes after hearing Tasker's calm words, and as he began to fly to Cold Bay, hairs began to rise on the back of Ratte's neck. Reality was setting in. Those men were out on the deck in survival suits because they knew the boat wasn't coming back from one of those rolls.

Parting with a vessel is a big thing for fishermen, but they were ready. What-ifs flew through Ratte's head. He asked for opinions from the crew. "What if we're 75 miles away getting gas at Cold Bay when that boat rolls over and goes down? What if six men die because the trained rescue people were there and didn't try?"

A lot of indecision followed. Then co-pilot Lieutenant Gene Rush said, "Hey, Paul, you gotta go with what your gut says. That's all you can do."

That's what Ratte wanted to hear. In his twelve years with search and rescue, one picture had lodged in his mind: a man floating away, face down, in a yellow slicker. Ratte had served on a cutter for eighteen months before flight school, and it was on the cutter that he had seen that sight. The thought that always accompanied his memory of that slicker was, "How could the Coast Guard have been in the vicinity for four hours, and the life of the person in the yellow slicker was still lost?" That case still figures in his risk management thoughts.

Before the actual rescue attempt, Captain Tasker had decided the order in which the men would leave the boat. First was a man with a child at home. Second was the panicky fellow. Tasker would be last.

Ratte radioed Tasker that they would have 45 minutes to complete the rescue and still have fuel enough for the trip back to Cold Bay. The plan was to drop to the deck an orange trail line about as thick as clothesline and weighted with three five-pound bags of lead shot. When someone on deck has it in hand, the line is clipped to the basket, which is also clipped to the hoist cable. The man below pulls the basket to him as the winch operator plays out the cable. A man gets in, and the crewman below plays out the trail line as the basket is hoisted to the chopper. Under ideal conditions, the trail line can be dropped straight down from the helicopter only once, and the basket process repeated until all have been rescued but the man handling the line on deck. By the time he climbs into the basket, he knows just what to expect.

By no means were these ideal conditions. The *Nowitna* was constantly moving under the force of wind and waves. The chopper was facing the boat's port side and into wild winds that jerked it about. Pilot Paul Ratte compared his job to holding a car to a gas pump in an earthquake. On top of that, he couldn't even see what was happening below him. Hoist operator Petty Officer John Overholt served as his eyes. Attached to a gunner's belt, Overholt was leaning out the door a foot or two, so he could see down. Constantly talking, he signaled the pilot to go up, down, right, left, forward or back, and indicated how many feet the pilot should move the aircraft in each direction. The problem was that there was a time delay between Overholt's seeing the need, his articulating it, and Ratte's hearing and reacting to it. Things were changing so fast that a new correction was needed before Ratte had time to fully react to the last one.

The rescuers in the helicopter were trying to stay about 90 feet above the boat, and the 105-foot trail line was too bowed by the wind to reach the deck. Overholt linked a second trail line onto the first, giving him 210 feet. The line was still bowing back under the helicopter, so Overholt would swing it into the wind and hope it landed in the right place. They had chosen to drop the weighted line onto the open deck between the wheelhouse and the crane. Instead, the changing variables took the line and weights spinning around the mast above the wheelhouse.

Captain Tasker came out of the wheelhouse dressed in his loose Gumby suit and heavy, clumsy rubber gloves, with his hood sometimes flapping over his eyes, and began a wild ride, climbing the 18-foot ladder welded to the mast. It's one thing to be on the deck of a ship or boat rolling back and forth. It's quite another to be climbing up a mast ladder where the length and speed of swing gets more drastic the higher you go. Also intensifying is the whipping action that's trying to throw you off when the mast reaches the end of the roll and suddenly reverses direction.

Had it not been for the "exact clarity" that can come in an extreme emergency—when there's no time to think out a plan, but you "know" precisely what needs to be done and suddenly have the power and focus that have allowed people to lift cars off the bodies of pinned victims—Tasker would have been much like a 205-pound lure being cast by a very stiff fishing rod. At one point, his feet were whipped off a ladder rung, and he was hanging onto another in trapeze fashion. Despite it all, he managed to get the weighted bags unwound from the mast.

Back in the wheelhouse, Thorne Tasker radioed the chopper, "Hey, guys, I'm an old fat man. Don't do that again." Everybody aboard the boat and the helicopter was highly stressed, and that comment lessened the gravity a bit. Not that it was true. Tasker is built stocky, but at forty-five years old, five-foot-ten, and 205 pounds, he was neither old nor fat.

Overholt tried another toss of the line, and this time it headed for the deck. A crewman reached for it, and would have had it, but at that moment the boat dropped into a trough and away from the line. Overholt recovered it before the bags could hang up on a rail or something else.

Wind gusts were whipping around at 60 to 70 knots. If Ratte got in position with a gust and it changed direction or speed, the chopper got knocked back or shot forward by 10 or 15 feet. Overholt also had to watch out for rogue waves that could shoot the boat high up enough to hit the helicopter. At one point, Tasker saw the mast hovering in the air 3 feet higher than the helicopter. If Ratte hadn't had the chopper far enough off to one side, the mast would have impaled it.

With the boat, chopper, waves, and winds all moving independently, it was impossible to say how the variables might come together to make a disaster out of Overholt's next swing of the trail line. Now it flew right back over the wheelhouse again. This time, the bags spun around a heavy stainless-steel ground wire for the single-sideband radio, setting up a challenge that would make Tasker's first climb look like child's play.

The mast and ladder went up though a catwalk of expanded metal about 12 feet long and positioned across the boat. Designed for around-the-clock fishing, high-pressure sodium lamps that look like at the ones that illuminate football fields were mounted in a framework up there.

They didn't last long, so they were maintained from the catwalk. A railing around it was just under chest height. The ground wire went down from under the port end of the catwalk at an angle to a corner of the wheelhouse.

Once more, Captain Tasker climbed the ladder, but not in his Gumby suit. After the first experience, he didn't want clumsy gloves or a suit loose enough to catch the wind. The Gumby suit is better designed to keep a man alive in that cold Bering Sea, but switching into a Mustang suit made him more agile. Tasker concluded that if the boat did cast him into the sea, the helicopter might get to him in time. If not, he was as good as dead no matter what he wore.

The *Nowitna* was drifting at about 5 knots, and the rudders and propellers were right in line with the spot into which Tasker would be pitched. Once the boat overtook him, he'd never survive being pummeled with the sharp edges of that equipment. The *Nowitna*'s violent 30-foot-plus rearing and bucking would make it worse.

Tasker crawled under the port end of the railing on his belly, but couldn't reach the weighted bags. He tried to somehow lock his knees on the railing's corner posts. That wasn't working well, and wouldn't get him far enough down the cable anyhow. Gripping the cable and spreading his legs against the corner posts of the catwalk, which was about 6 inches wider than his hips, he pulled himself down until he could hook his ankles on the posts. This was the sort of move only an acrobat could pull off on dry land, and it took another dose of "exact clarity" for the captain to get into that precarious position and have the strength to stay there as the boat's violent rolling tried to sling him off.

Unfortunately, he was still inches from reaching the weighted bags. Incredibly, Tasker let go with his right ankle. He was not only able to hang on with his left hand and one ankle, he managed to reach out with his right hand and slap the bags to unwind them from the cable. To scoot back up, he timed the rolls. When the boat was returning from starboard and entering the port part of the roll, he felt more weightless.

At the instant the port roll stopped to reverse itself, the jolt severely tried to pitch him. Hitting the starboard reversal produced a jolt in a helpful direction.

After this, Ratte and Overholt decided to move the rescue attempts to the bow. This position allowed Ratte to see the *Nowitna*'s stern in his peripheral vision, which eliminated some of the time delays between Overholt's instructions and Ratte's reactions.

One by one, the boat crew timed the rolls so seas weren't washing across the deck, and then raced to the bow. Twice the weighted bags swung too far forward of the bow and missed. Ratte moved a bit toward the stern, and after another couple tries, a crew member grabbed the line. Number one, the fisherman with a child at home, was winched to the chopper. The crewman still had hold of the line and kept it taut as the basket came down. Number two, the panicky guy, went up.

On the third try, Overholt had been "conning" Ratte to get the helicopter directly above the basket, so that as it ascended, it would hang like a plumb line below the chopper. That's essential to keep the basket from swinging. Just then, the *Nowitna* dropped into a trough, leaving the basket in the air to unexpectedly swing in a wide arc that took it all the way around the structure holding the forward lights. When Overholt saw the basket clear the hazards, he maxed the winch speed and hauled the guy up. The trailing line with the weights, however, caught somewhere and popped the weak link at the basket. That weak link releases at 300 pounds of pressure to prevent the chopper from ever becoming tied to the boat.

Overholt had another 105-foot trail line, but no more bags of lead shot. Swimmer Bob Watson emptied a nylon helmet bag and put some wheel chocks in as weights. Too light. When lowered out the door, it flew back to the chopper's tail. Watson looked around and added a fire extinguisher. The first drop didn't make it far enough onto the boat. It slid into the sea, but the bag filled with water, adding weight that made the next try perfect. The fourth man was hoisted easily.

Captain Tasker had listed himself as last, but the crewman who had been tending the trail line, a Samoan, considered himself practiced at the job by now. Also, knowing what the captain had been through, the crewman didn't think the captain should be last. Tasker went. Somehow a lot of swinging ensued, yanking the trail line from the sixth, last man's hands and off the boat. Ratte saw it and thought, "Boy, that guy has to feel lonely down there. Now we gotta start all over again to get him."

The Samoan was standing in the forward area on a vessel with a bow sinking ever deeper, a boat that could go down at any moment. When it did, the suction would pull him down with it. He knew only that the trail line and the makeshift weight bag got away from him. With the sky dark and stormy, he couldn't tell if it was lost. Nor could he know whether the rescuers had anything else that might be used as a makeshift weight bag—or even if they had another line. He did know that the chopper would have a swimmer, and he knew he wanted away from the *Nowitna*. Only those giant waves made him hesitate about jumping in.

The boat was being driven sideways at about 5 knots. Jumping from the port side, he'd be overtaken and go under the boat. Jumping off the starboard side, the waves would hold him against the *Nowitna*. Maybe he could go off the bow—if he could make headway swimming across that kind of wave action.

As Captain Tasker climbed out of the basket, the view from the chopper showed him that the *Nowitna*'s situation was even more grave than he had thought it was when aboard.

Overholt breathed a sigh of relief. The line was still attached to the basket, and the weight bag hadn't ripped off on a railing. He could con Ratte back over the boat for a quick and successful drop. There wasn't room in the helicopter for the basket and the sixth man separately, but the Samoan was happy to stay in it for the ride back to Cold Bay.

Nobody had eaten for many hours, but they weren't complaining. Lieutenant Gene Rush, co-pilot, had grabbed a bag of lollipops to stave off hunger and offered them to the fishermen. Each took one and then, exhausted, fell asleep for the rest of the 45-minute flight back.

When they landed, the fuel level was about 15 minutes from triggering the "Bingo" light. When that light goes on, the chopper leaves to refuel, no matter what's happening.

According to vessels in the vicinity, the *Nowitna* went down shortly after the rescue.

(See this book's Introduction for astounding proof of how powerful the mind, or at least Tasker's, can be.)

# 13

*Author Larry Mueller believes he survived a charging wild boar unscathed because, in an extreme emergency, the conscious brain has no time to reason. You don't even have time to be afraid. Rather, the subconscious computes an instant picture of what you need to do.*

NOWHERE TO RUN, nowhere to hide. I'm on a bare gravel river beach with a wild boar charging straight at me. My buddies can't get to a weapon fast enough, and I'm armed with a camera. In seconds, that boar is 4 feet in front of me.

You have to know the characters involved to understand how I got into this mess. T. E. "Tom" Scott had built his dog supply manufacturing business into one that made millions annually, and I suppose he had become a wealthy eccentric. I knew him earlier, when he was still a working eccentric.

Texas hunting lodge owner Roy Wilson didn't know Tom at all until he found himself next door to him in a sports show booth. Tom had all of his new model beeper collars turned on, and was hawking his wares above the din. Roy's complaint about the noise elicited two suggestions from Tom.

"You could buy all my beepers and turn them off," Tom suggested, "or I might tone it down for an invitation to hunt quail."

Incredibly, Tom got his invitation to hunt on Wilson's Crooked Creek Outfitters holdings. Unfortunately for me, he also learned about a herd of wild hogs—Europeans, ferals, and crosses—on the property.

"Barefoot Bob" Richardson, then a camp guide with a day job fighting Abilene fires, put excitement into his life by hunting wild boars with yellow blackmouth curs. Tom figured I couldn't resist an adventure like that and arranged a mid-January hunt.

In the meantime, I came down with a fever that three different antibiotics failed to touch. The fourth one worked, but took another twenty-one days. Now it was March 1. I was missing ten pounds, weak as a willow, and hunting something as well-mannered and gentle as hogs, with somebody as well-mannered and gentle as T. E. Scott.

Fortunately, another quail guide, Allen Moeller, was along with a second pickup. Bob and Tom would start the dogs upriver. Allen and I would drive a mile upstream and watch for pigs sneaking through.

Allen's tires were barely rolling when the dogs bawled loudly about a jumped hog across Crooked Creek from us. Allen wheeled the pickup around, bounced over the rocky ford, narrowly missed bottoming out on a huge boulder, and spun tires up the opposite bank.

When we caught up to the pack, the hog bailed off into the water. The bank wasn't very high right there—maybe 3 or 4 feet—but it was straight up-and-down. The dogs piled in with the hog, and since it couldn't climb out, it churned across the creek to a gravel beach. Allen did his driving performance in reverse and got us there just as the dogs were trying to wrest the beachhead from a hog determined to chase his attackers back into the drink.

Boars usually set up defense in brush too thick for shooting quality pictures, so this was such an unbelievably perfect photo op that it must have overstimulated me. I was well-prepared, with a fairly new computerized 35 mm Canon EOS with auto focus for anything moving, motor drive, automatic rewind, and a feature to preset for adequate shutter speed, so that I could avoid blurred action shots while the camera automatically adjusted the lens opening to compensate for changing light. All I had to worry about was picture composition and staying with the action. And the action was extremely fast-paced and constantly changing, with hounds all over that boar and that boar quite capable of holding its own against anything the dogs tried. In no time at all, I had thirty-six shots. Then the automatic rewind kicked in, and I was seeing one missed great shot after another, and wondering how many more I would miss before I could get reloaded.

Suddenly Tom was behind me, sarcastically asking, "Have you ever done this before?" He claimed the rewind hadn't stopped before I opened the camera and started pulling on film as if I were field-dressing a rabbit. I couldn't believe it. He was right. A large part of the roll was yanked out, exposed to the light, and ruined. Obviously, my attention had been entirely on the fight while I tried to quickly reload without looking. Then the boar jumped into Crooked Creek and swam to the other side to escape the dogs, who were having none of that. They were right behind him.

Once again, the boar was corralled by the high bank, but the yellow blackmouth curs had their own problems. On solid ground, these agile descendants of Spanish *perros de sange* ("dogs of blood") that Hernando De Soto had scattered across the South could dance away from the boar's tusks. In water, everything including dodging tusks has to be done in slow motion, so the curs kept a respectful distance.

Further slowing this naval engagement was the medieval-style armor of gristle that, under the skin, covers the neck and shoulders of European wild boars. While it protects against predators and bad-tempered other hogs, this armor gives a boar a very rigid front end. Wild boars can't flex around to protect their flanks, as most other animals whose teeth are their weapons can do.

Finally, one dog in the pack—a dog that was somewhat different from the others—threw caution to the winds. The water happened to be cold. The air temperature hovered around 32 degrees, and slick-ice covered the rocks. Barefoot Bob's slender little thin-coated blue Lacey stock dog, a breed rarely seen outside of Texas, could take it no longer. She slipped in from behind and crawled on top of the boar's head.

In a blink, the boar sunk like the *Titanic*, somehow sucking his passenger along. Just as quickly, Bob was on his way across the ford in hopes of saving his dog. As I watched, the blue Lacey surfaced, but the boar remained under. At last, very cautiously, the boar's nose emerged, followed slowly by the rest of the head. Oddly, it was coming straight up. This large-bodied, tiny-hoofed animal had managed to stay down and swim under water—against the current!—for 15 feet. The blue Lacey now kept its distance, concluding that shivering was safer than warming up on a hog. But the gritty little dog didn't desert the pack and go AWOL on land. It stayed in the water.

The boar looked for its adversaries, but unable to swivel its head, and not thinking to turn around, it persistently peered in the wrong direction, giving the dogs time to close in from behind. Surprised, "Titanic" led the flotilla of wannabe destroyers back to the beach.

On land, the boar's charges heightened in ferocity, inciting the yellow curs to take unwise risks too close to the tusks. Once again, the battle returned to the water, and still the blue Lacey did not desert. True to his name, Barefoot Bob kicked off his boots and ran behind, determined not to give that boar another chance to drown dogs. Fifteen feet out, a drop-off left Bob swimming behind the dogs, who were swimming behind the hog in hypothermically frigid water.

Bob's human presence made the dogs too brave and aggressive for the circumstances, but the melee swung the boar's rear end toward Bob. He grabbed the tail and held on to become Titanic's rudder. He could now steer his craft back to the beach. Bob found river bottom footing sooner than the boar could, of course, and grabbed the right ear while his left hand still held the tail. I stared in wonder as this hog wrestler suddenly switched from his ear/tail grip to grabbing both hind legs at the hocks and wheelbarrowing the boar onto the beach. A quick flip, and the boar was on its side, held down by Bob's right knee while he hog-tied the four feet.

Up close, Titanic didn't fit the name. He was a European/feral cross not quite large enough to be a suitable herd sire, and too old to be mild in flavor. Every Texan knows the cut that makes a boar fit to eat the next time he's caught, so this hog got a temporary reprieve along with a swift slice that ended his amorous adventures forever. It was also the final insult. That hog was walleyed, maniacally mad!

I had just made that observation, in fact, when Bob, red as a radish from the icy water, and still standing barefoot on frozen ground, asked, "Larry, have you ever photographed a charging boar? When I turn him loose, he'll run down the beach past the trucks. Stand in the middle, and you'll get a great picture."

My look made clear that I questioned his sanity, which was already in doubt after the Tarzan-like river episode. "Oh," he assured me, "we'll pull a truck up behind you. When the hog gets too close, jump aboard."

That sounded like just the amount of excitement my weakened condition could tolerate. I set up shop on the beach and waited for Allen to deliver the truck. Suddenly, I realized he hadn't gotten the message, and yet Bob was cutting loose the boar. Here it came, just as predicted.

The last time I got in the way of a hog, it had crossed a Louisiana bayou to lose dogs and was running straight at me. It didn't look all that close through my viewfinder, but my buddy was yelling, "Get back to the airboat!" I looked up. The hog was 50 feet in front of me, the boat 50 feet behind. If I ran, this sow would chase. I'd be caught anyway, so I took another picture. The hog stopped, perhaps bluffed out because I didn't run. Could I get a replay of that here in Texas?

Strangely, this situation didn't overexcite me like that first fight on the beach. I calmly, but quickly, centered the viewfinder's auto-focus mark on the boar's forehead and started the motor drive—expecting a half dozen shots. I got just two before the hog was almost on me. This boar wouldn't be bluffed. What now?

There was no time for my brain to reason out a plan. It didn't have time to tell me to be afraid, either, so I wasn't. I also suspect that in a sudden and extreme emergency, the subconscious computes independently, and delivers a crisp, wordless mental printout.

In that final split second, I got the picture. Suddenly I just "knew" that something as stiffnecked as a European wild boar couldn't turn on a dime—but that, at the same time, if it was given enough distance, it could easily execute an adequate turn. I'd have to stand poised until the very last possible moment. At 4 feet, I launched into a world-class side jump. The boar whizzed by while I was still airborne, and I landed, turning with the hog to see if I'd have to do this over again.

No, the boar was now chasing Tom, who was racing for a truck in a most peculiar form of running. His head was turned slightly back, one eye apparently calculating the nearness of the boar, the other scanning forward to avoid tripping. Bob released a cur, which distracted the boar, but the boar promptly chased off the dog and sent all three of my friends jumping onto trucks.

I was able to glory in asking them why they all let a little thing like a wild boar chase them around that way. It was especially glorious because I was beginning to suspect that this may have been more than a photo shoot—it might have been a setup so they could have a little rough-house fun with the writer, and it backfired. I didn't need the truck they failed to place behind me, and they all needed one badly. They denied a conspiracy and stuck with their story, so I still don't know for sure. But whatever took place there, I had all the fun.

# 14

*Neither man would survive if severely injured John Weiland did not keep trying to find new ways to overcome extreme obstacles.*

CLIMBERS John Weiland, forty-seven, and Brian Teale, thirty-seven, were beneath a 12-foot half-bell of ice in Keystone Canyon north of Valdez, Alaska, when Teale saw a small crack widen. His warning shout was drowned out by a loud explosion, as ice ranging in size from marbles to half-ton blocks flew in every direction. A huge chunk crushed twelve of Teale's ribs. His punctured lung gurgled. He could only whisper, "I'm dying." Another block smashed Weiland's left ankle and hyperflexed his right knee. Yet another broke his left leg in two places. Fighting blackout from pain and shock, Weiland knew that they both would die if he didn't get help.

This was the sort of thing that shouldn't have happened to these men. Both had reputations for never falling, never getting hurt. Weiland was credited with bringing ice climbing to the region. He ran an ice-climbing school for fifteen years. He scaled the six-rated Wowie Zowie icefall, a giant 400-foot icicle hanging from the lip of an overhanging cliff, when the "dead-dash vertical" upper section had become honeycombed. Bob Shelton took a plunge on that climb when surface ice peeled away. His rope yanked out the first ice screw, but the second one held. The belaying device at John's end of the rope stopped Shelton's fall.

Teale guided one of Japan's best climbers up Wowie Zowie. The visitor is reported to have said that there were no such climbs in his country, and if there were, he wouldn't attempt it. For Brian, with twenty years of experience, and John with thirty, the Hung Jury ice bells would be a fairly routine climb.

Keystone Canyon is an 800-foot-deep slash across the Chugach Range. The canyon forms a natural two-and-a-half-mile wind tunnel. Winds this day were 60 to 70 miles per hour. With the temperature at 5 degrees, wind chills were around 30 below.

Over fifty frozen waterfalls hang from the canyon walls. During summer, water emerges springlike from the sides of the canyon and runs off into the Lowe River. By November, the falls begin to freeze into formations of exquisite beauty, offering great challenges to climbers. At Hung Jury, the wind goes around a corner and blows upward, suspending the water and pushing it away from the wall. As it freezes, it begins to form ice bells, actually half-bells, that are perhaps 6 feet thick at the base and extend outward as much as 15 to 18 feet. At the end, the thickness may narrow to inches. Hung Jury is a series of such bells. The challenge to climbers is to weave their way up the icy grooves. On a scale of one to six, Hung Jury is considered a four in terms of difficulty and skill required.

Access to the ice formation is simple. Drive north out of Valdez on the Richardson Highway to mile 13, cross the frozen Lowe River, and almost stroll up the 45-degree slope, right below a spectacular formation that can be easily seen from the highway. The "technical climb" began when the men neared Hung Jury.

The slope directly below the nearest bell was covered with ice, a part of the frozen waterfall. Weiland and Teale avoided that. Only ¼ to ½ inch thick, the ice could easily chip away under crampon spikes and cause a fall. The ascent was safer on the hard-packed snow to the right of the ice.

Climbing to a level with the bell, the men then traversed to the left until they reached the "ledge" beneath the ice overhang. This was a ledge only in ice-climber vernacular, however. Climbers also "stand" on vertical ice when most people would consider what they're doing to be clinging by ice axes and toe spikes. This ledge was actually a depression in the ice that caused a cavelike space beneath the bell. Nowhere was the floor anywhere near level. It was simply less steep than its surroundings. To sit on it would have invited a slide into eternity.

As they entered the cave under this 12-foot bell, Brian looked up and commented that the bell was cracked. "Might fall," John answered, mostly in jest. Climbers see lots of cracked ice. And this was January. Winter ice, though easy to chip, rarely falls apart in large pieces.

Ice, however, has a life of its own. There's a transition from brittle at 10 below zero to rather plastic at 10 or 15 above. The ax will shatter brittle ice, but sink in easily when it's plastic. While the surface may be brittle during winter, the bells don't ordinarily break up until April.

Brian moved to the back of the cave and fastened an ice screw into the wall. The rope went through the screw eye to his waist. The other end of the 300-foot rope went through John's harness and back to Brian's belaying device. John would step off to the left of the ledge onto the vertical ice and go straight up, assuming the task of lead climber. Brian would come second as the belayer. He would handle the rope through the device that would stop John if he fell.

Brian was 4 feet from John, who was now stepping off the ledge with his left foot. His right foot was still on the ledge with the right leg bent at the knee while the left foot reached down to gain purchase on the ice with the toe spikes.

At that moment, Brian saw the crack widen. The ice moved and he screamed, "Johnny!" But the word was drowned out by the explosion of tons of ice blasting apart under the force of some unknown stress. The bell showered down on the men in pieces of all sizes. One huge hunk hit Brian, crushing his chest and knocking him into Johnny. In the next instant, a big block from above struck Johnny's left ankle, shattering the boot, smashing the ankle, tearing the ligaments, and driving him downward with such force that it hyperflexed his right knee and bent his right crampon.

A half second later, another immense chunk struck Johnny between the knee and the foot of the left leg, breaking the fibula in two places. "Brian!" he screamed. And at that moment a 5- by 2- by 2-foot block hit the ledge on end, tilted back, then dropped on Brian's chest and John's left arm, effectively pinning both men.

With bigger hells to deal with, neither man was quite aware of the pummeling and bruising their bodies continued to receive from marble-sized fragments still blowing around in the 60- to 70-mile-per-hour winds. Weiland could hear gurgling in Teal's chest and knew it meant a punctured lung. Brian was on his back and pinned against John, still tied to the rope he had just fastened. John was on the rim of the ledge with his right foot up and his left arm trapped under the ice block. His left hand still gripped the ice ax driven into the sloping floor of the once bell-like cave.

Weakened though his right leg was, Weiland nevertheless maintained a purchase with his right foot. He pushed and shoved against the block of ice. Although terribly heavy, it was at least tilted. If he could further shift its balance, it might roll off. Teal did what he could to help. Aided by adrenaline, desperation, and a few minutes of determined "if this doesn't work, try something else," they managed to move the block enough to change its center of gravity. It slid away.

John shifted Brian enough to get his head higher than his body, and in that position tied him to another ice screw. Morphine was in his pack, but that was under the deep pile of ice rubble.

John looked over the rim of the small ledge. The icefall, or frozen waterfall, was 30 feet straight down. Below that, the glazed canyon wall fell away at a 45-degree angle. Weiland pulled on the rope, trying to get enough length to lower himself. It wouldn't budge from under the rubble. He unsnapped the rope from his harness. With or without it, he had to get down.

Normally, ice climbers spider up and down vertical faces with ice axes in each hand and crampons on their boots. John still had the axes. Six-inch steel spikes are mounted on 16-inch handles. Cleverly curved to the arc of the swing, these picks hold considerable weight when properly driven into ice.

Crampons, meanwhile, clamp onto hard plastic boots. Ten spikes point downward from them to grip the ice. Two more spikes stick out from the toes, to be kicked into vertical ice. The climber is always connected to the ice by three of his limbs while he moves the fourth.

Unfortunately, John's left boot was smashed. The sole was gone. So was the crampon. Of course, that was academic, because his broken left leg and smashed ankle weren't functional anyway. Weiland tried to move over the edge, only to learn that the bent crampon on his right boot had fallen off. Again, it was academic, because his right knee was so badly sprung that he couldn't possibly kick spikes into the ice. Nothing was left but his two ice axes and the knowledge that with one slip he would fall into a deadly uncontrolled ride down the 45-degree slope.

But Brian was dying. Mustering his great arm strength despite fighting nausea and shock, John drove the first ax into the ice and hung on with one hand. The second ax went in somewhat lower so he could hang on with the other hand and pull the first ax free to move it farther down. Little by little, he lowered himself down the wall, then used the axes to painfully crab to the left of the 45-degree icefall at the bottom. Finally, he reached the hard snow slope. On his stomach, descending feet-first, he could now control his rate of slide in a one-step-at-a-time fashion with the ice axes.

On the other hand, he couldn't see what was ahead. Despite the shock-induced numbing that was allowing him to move at all, it was excruciatingly painful every time his left leg hit a bump or a bush sticking out of the ice and snow.

John tried rolling onto his back. That made it more difficult to use the axes, but at least he could avoid obstacles. Driving the ax heads into the snowpack one at a time beside his hips, he slowly descended 150 yards, stopping above the river at an elevation overlooking the highway.

Trying to cross the Lowe River would be too risky. Of all places in Keystone Canyon, the wind is strongest on the river. It could easily blow him across the ice and sweep him into one of the big holes kept open by the current. He waited.

Richardson Highway comes around a bend that leaves drivers facing the canyon wall, and nobody can resist looking at the ice bells. In the very first car to show up was a pair of gutsy snowboarders, who pursue a sport best described as skiing on surfboards. Donny Mills, sixteen, and Miles Burgett, twenty-two, saw Weiland in his orange parka, waving and yelling. They stopped and listened, but couldn't understand him from 150 yards across the river. The young men did, however, recognize the urgent need for a rescue team. They raced to town and alerted the Valdez volunteer team members along with Dr. Andrew Embick, a hard-core climber heavily involved in the annual Valdez Ice Climbing Festival.

Mills and Burgett immediately drove back and walked across the river without crampons, despite the danger from extreme winds. Burgett sat beside Weiland to break the biting wind. Donny Mills not only ascended the 45-degree slope of snowpack without crampons, he somehow negotiated the icefall to reach Brian Teale.

"I think that was the most daredevil feat of the rescue," Weiland said later. "I don't know how he accomplished it without a fall. He sheltered Brian from the marble-size ice still blowing around. But just somebody being there and assuring Brian that the rescue team was coming probably saved his life. I know what it meant to have Miles there with me. I was drifting in and out of a semilucid state. Later, a hunter stopped and came over to wrap a sleeping bag around me."

The rescue team exercised more caution. They anchored ropes across the river. There would be several men on the ice at one time when they brought the victims back across. They couldn't risk breaking through or losing someone to the wind.

Dr. Embick climbed up to Brian, along with firemen/EMTs Dave Gildersleeve and Joe Loffredo. The wind was so intense that even the backboard designed for mountain rescue was lifted off the ice. Everything had to be tied down. A visiting Fairbanks anesthesiologist, Dr. Randall McGregor, also an ice climber, tended to John Weiland.

Gildersleeve and Loffredo lowered Teale on a 600-foot rope. Dr. Embick, attached to Teale's backboard by a rope, rappelled down the slope ahead of him. Only when in the ambulance did Dr. Embick dare to cut the frozen clothes off Brian. At the hospital, it took two-and-a-half hours to halt bleeding, restore normal breathing, and prepare him for the flight to Providence Hospital in Anchorage.

John Weiland said he was put back together "with a thousand screws" that fastened the ligaments and bones of his ankle and leg in place. The pain was so intense for the first two weeks that morphine couldn't touch it. His leg had to be lengthened with coral and steel to accomplish a correct gait.

How did Brian and John show their appreciation and gratitude for their rescue and restoration? Probably the way Drs. Embick and McGregor would have. Both men went back to ice climbing. "When something is a part of you," Weiland said, "you stay with it."

# 15

*Mike Harbaugh asked for a miracle, then ingeniously helped himself while waiting for it to come on wings from the 71st Aerospace Rescue & Recovery Squadron.*

ALMOST as soon as the sky cleared that Sunday, Mike Harbaugh, thirty-four, a Wasilla plumbing contractor, secured the heavily loaded red-and-white Cessna 182, climbed into the cockpit, and revved the engine.

"Storm's moved past. We'd better get going," he shouted to his long-time friend, the Reverend Glen Johnson, a retired Assembly of God minister who sat at the controls of a newer-model Cessna 182 on the Flat airstrip, 300 miles northwest of Anchorage.

Both pilots had waited out three days of bad weather for safe flying. Neither wanted to dare the treacherous Merrill Pass, with its sharp turns, razor peaks, and mysterious wind shears, except under the best of conditions. Now, on February 9, 1986, came a break in the weather, and the two planes, loaded with Johnson's household goods, took off for Soldotna, on the other side of the mountains.

What seemed like ideal conditions in the pass soon changed. Harbaugh found himself fighting the fiercest winds he'd encountered in nine years of Alaska flying. Johnson's faster plane had long since disappeared into the distance. Now there was an added irritation: Harbaugh was aware of Johnson's hearing problems. Even so, he tried to radio Johnson's plane. No response.

As blinding snow cycloned over the windshield like bursts of confetti in a wind tunnel, Harbaugh prayed, "Please, God, get me through."

Battling the headwind was taking all the skill Harbaugh could muster. His fingers tightened on the controls as he figured his next move. He knew he was approaching Razors Edge, a section of the pass flanked with peaks as high as 12,000 feet. He scanned the instrument panel, and stared down at the perpendicular terrain boxing him in. Below, where the pass narrowed into a ragged bottleneck, was wreckage-strewn terrain that had already claimed fourteen crash victims, the latest only a month before. A landing attempt anywhere would be sheer suicide.

"Better do a 180," he told himself aloud. "Spend the night on a mountain lake someplace."

Death had brushed Mike Harbaugh once before at Razors Edge, back in 1984. Then, as now, he had only one option—altitude. With the stall indicator going haywire, Harbaugh had tried to pull out of a 180 with the same difficulty, that time carrying a ten-year-old passenger. "Looks like we're going down, son," he said. But somehow they hadn't crashed. For months, Harbargh felt Providence had intervened. But this time he might have been running out of luck.

"Please God," he cried. "Keep her up—up."

His best course, he figured, was to continue through the turn as tight as he could. He began banking through punishing winds. Then a shattering burst of energy—a "wind shear"—struck, tossing the craft like a maple leaf in an autumn gale. Harbaugh lurched forward in his seat. Shifting crates smashed against the side of the Cessna. A generator anchored to the floor groaned against its harness. The steeply tilting plane began sliding. Harbaugh screamed, "God, am I going to . . . ?" as the plane plummeted uncontrollably in the direction of the steep incline.

Paralyzed and helpless, Harbaugh saw serrated rocks just moments before the crash.

The aircraft disintegrated. Harbaugh was knocked unconscious.

He had no idea how long he lay sprawled on the slope. He remembered only the canopy of gray dusk yawning above him. When he opened his eyes he felt for his face and saw his hand come back bearing a sheen of blood. Even so, he felt triumph at having survived. I'm alive! Thank God for that! But for minutes he fought a memory block, and couldn't remember where he had been.

All his survival gear except a pair of coveralls, a jacket-hood, and mittens had been swept over a cliff. Agonizing pain tingled along his face and shoulders. He struggled to his knees and tried to stand. His body toppled and started to roll.

Frantically, he clawed at the rocky slope to brake his downward motion. Now, feeling terror and despair, he looked up at the peaks and down at the canyon. Some 30 to 50 feet away, he spotted a piece of the plane's tail assembly. Shelter!

His foot and ankle appeared to be badly broken. He fought to walk, jerking along his left leg. On hands and knees he crawled painfully to a mound of clothing in the snow. He struggled with the coveralls, inching them over his injured body, then put on the coat hood and mittens. Desperately, he worked his elbows into the snow-blown, rocky earth, dragging himself toward the torn segment of wreckage. Dizzy, his strength exhausted, he lay down next to the piece of fuselage. Three hours later he awakened, cold, bleeding, and in shock.

Gotta get inside. Harbaugh worried he might freeze. He found an air mattress near the plane fragment, stuffed it through the jagged opening of the tail section, and wriggled inside. Once in the dark interior, withering cold and raging thirst seized him.

"Help me!" he called aloud. "God, help me!"

Again, blackness claimed him.

The next day he awakened to darkness. His swollen, blood-filled eyes kept sticking shut. He had to sit very still and painfully work open one eye or the other with his hands. His collarbone, he surmised, was badly broken and he wondered whether he would ever be able to walk again on his left leg. Strewn around him on the snow like bloodstains were shattered chunks of his red-and-white Cessna.

He quickly discovered two more items: a cardboard box containing cups, a dish, rags, and a pair of socks; and the plane's baggage door. He planned to use the door to cover the opening in his shelter to protect himself from the snow.

Painfully, he crawled 50 feet downhill toward the door and propped himself against it, massaging his throbbing shoulder. He dropped his body to the earth stiffly, resting, preparing to shove it up the hill to his shelter. He lay back, physically drained from the exertion.

He prayed. How many hours before he'd be missed? Was his ELT (Emergency Locator Transmitter) in the tail section sending out signals? Without power there was no way to tell. Head down, choking, gasping, groaning, he forced the door forward once more, feeling his heart beating rapidly.

Don't pass out. God, give me strength. Gotta get that door up there.

During the next half hour, he moved the door uphill, then again crawled inside the tailpiece. Blood from his torn face kept clogging his throat when he tried to swallow.

That blood woke him hours later. It was snowing hard. Nothing could be worse, he thought. The snow will cover everything. There's no chance rescuers could spot me in this blizzard.

He groaned. His left foot was white and hard. His face ached. He could not twist or raise his body without pain. By mid-morning, thirst consumed him. He avoided eating snow, knowing that would hasten hypothermia.

*Unless I get water soon, I'll die,* he thought. He was near tears. Since the crash, he had consumed only a few tablespoons of water, produced by holding a cup of snow against his chest. Blood trickling from face wounds brought a salty taste to his mouth, intensifying his thirst. His throat ached. For a moment it didn't seem real—dying of thirst surrounded by wet snow. He had to have relief. Anything. He prayed earnestly, spontaneously, the way his mother, the Reverend Nola Harbaugh, an ordained minister and Evangelism Department employee, had prayed at her cancer diagnosis: "God, give me a miracle." Her prayers, her church felt, had transformed the cancer to a benign state. Then she had miraculously healed.

"God, you helped her," he called. "Now, help me."

Almost as if in reply to his prayer, he saw a battered generator in the crushed baggage compartment of the tail section. That was the answer! There was fuel in the generator. And he had matches.

He decided against draining fuel onto the plane floor. He had to find another way. Then he remembered the dish. Should he find enough fuel in the generator, he could drain it and start a blaze—but where could he get the wood?

By noon he was praying in seriousness: "God, you've given me matches and gasoline. What to burn?" Once more he looked around. His mind seemed to float away from the scene as it wished for a log, then it would return to stare in an odd way at the box. The box had been wrapped with layers of heavy plastic tape. He dug a knife from his pocket and cut up the box, arranging a pile of inch-wide cardboard pieces. Within minutes he would have warmth.

He twisted his body, crawled to the generator, and drained fuel into the dish. He struck a match. Nothing. Then the rest of the matches. No flame. They were wet. In the icy gray afternoon, his hopes plummeted. He crawled back inside the tailpiece to rest.

Suddenly he saw the plane's battery case. He wrapped a wire from positive to negative terminals, producing a shooting spark that set fire to a small piece of gas-soaked cardboard. He jammed snow into a crockery cup and held it to the fire until it melted. He seized the cup and gulped down the drink. Pain shot through his fingertips and mouth. Now, on top of everything else, he was suffering painful burns to his lips. Despairing, he lowered his head in his palms and wept.

All that evening he prayed, "God, please!"

Early the next morning Harbaugh kindled another small fire and melted more snow, soaking small pieces of rags in gas to keep it going. In the long hours that followed, strange doubts and fears began to bedevil him. Visions of being buried forever in the snow haunted him. Tortured by intermittent stabs of pain, he faded in and out of deep sleep.

Since he had crashed, a dozen small planes had flown high overhead in the pass. Now, as one approached, he waved his hand to attract attention. He was delirious with hope when the plane circled and came back. Then, the sound of the throbbing motors faded into silence. Within a few hours, another plane skimmed over him. Harbaugh was sure the pilot had seen him. The plane circled the mountain twice. Then it too drifted away to be swallowed in silence.

It will come back. It will. But he worried that he would not be alert enough to wave. He fought to stay watchful. He wanted rest, but commanded himself to listen for the throb of a chopper. Several hours later he imagined he heard the drone of engines—to no avail.

He was learning to parry each disappointment with a childlike prayer: "Lord, I know they're on the way. I know it."

Once more he scanned the skies, but when five hours had slipped away, he took stock. If his ELT were working, beeper-distress signals would have been picked up, and rescue planes would be crisscrossing the skies. But none were. That meant his survival mechanism was dead. As daylight faded that Tuesday, the temptation to despair was fast overwhelming Harbaugh. From somewhere inside he heard the words:

"Mike—you'd be dead now if God wanted you to die. You're already spared. Only a few hours more. Planes are on the way." Trying hard to believe, he closed his eyes and dozed off.

But by daybreak the next day, the cruelest blow struck. Harbaugh could no longer crawl out of his tailpiece. His hands had become bloated stumps. His legs were robbed of feeling. He was unable to twist his body either way in the shelter. Even waving was difficult. It had been nearly three full days since he had hit the mountain. Now fighting hopelessness, he managed to sing a hymn—something he had learned back at Sunday school in Indiana.

Thinking about his family helped erase his growing despair. He concentrated on his wife, Linda, their son, Gabriel, five, and their combined children from previous marriages—Donna, eighteen; Mike, fifteen; Theresa, thirteen; Becky, eleven. He basked in the memory of last Christmas with Linda's new grandson, Shawn. Would there be any more Christmases?

Then, with a shudder, he thought he heard something—or someone—walking outside the tailpiece. Was he hallucinating? He knew this part of Alaska was infested with bears known to attack humans. If it was a bear, merciful death would come soon.

"God, make it go away," he prayed.

He tried to convince himself that what he heard was only the wind, that rescuers were already trying to find him. All his life, he reminded himself, the Lord had been forgiving and good. All he needed to do was have faith, lie back, and wait. But it was essential that he fight to stay awake—to keep from drifting off at all costs. What frightened him most was the fear of drifting into death.

Mike Harbaugh's disappearance touched off a massive search spearheaded by Civil Air Patrol and Alaska State Patrol aircraft and assisted by dozens of volunteer pilots, including the Reverend Johnson who had turned and headed out of the pass to escape the winds.

After struggling in vain to spot Harbaugh, Johnson landed at a small village and telephoned rescuers. On the third day of the massive search, an HC-130 Kingbird commanded by Captain Bryan Lillegard, pilot, took off for Merrill Pass at 9 A.M. It looked like a routine search day. The Kingbird would fly high over the pass, coordinating the search with thirteen small aircraft while keeping an alert for any ELT signals.

Nine hours of search yielded nothing. Then, a private pilot told authorities he had glimpsed what appeared to be a survivor waving his hand in the Razors Edge area. A similar sighting was reported by a Civil Air Patrol pilot. At 6:30 P.M. on February 12, the phone jangled in the Rescue Coordination Center at Elmendorf Air Force Base. Major Merrill Perrine gulped in disbelief at what he was told by the caller. "Incredible!" he exclaimed. "Out there on the mountain for three days in freezing weather! We'll scramble right away."

Perrine knew no time could be lost. By telephone he told the 71st Aerospace Rescue & Recovery Squadron, "We've got to have a helicopter and crew. We've got a crash survivor down on Merrill Pass. He's badly injured but still alive. Has to be a night rescue. Otherwise . . ."

Chopper Pilot Captain Scott Sommer agreed. They had to move immediately. Every hour counted. A veteran of 2,100 hours of flying time, Sommer had picked up three bodies on the same mountain a month before. He ordered para-rescuers Sergeant Ryan J. Beckmann and Airman First Class Patrick Keller to load picks, axes, a bolt cutter, and medical packs. "We'll need them," he said.

"We will," Beckmann said, "if he's alive."

As the helicopter crew—Sommer, Beckmann, Keller, Second Lieutenant Kevin Churchill, co-pilot, and Sergeant Richard Proctor II, flight engineer—launched off runway 33, the Kingbird, piloted by Lillegard, returned to refuel and load extra night illumination flares.

A fatiguing day of fruitless search told on the faces of the Kingbird crew: Lillegard; Captain James Hickin, co-pilot; First Lieutenant

Robert A. Palmer, navigator; Sergeant Kenneth Griffin, radio man; Sergent Frederick Manning and Senior Airman Eric Johnson, para-rescuers (PJs); Sergeant Jeff Wheat, flight engineer; and Senior Airman Bradley Brown, loadmaster.

Inside the chopper, Sommer briefed his men. They would take the helicopter into the black belly of the pass. From this precarious perch inside towering walls of rock, they'd scan the low slopes for Harbaugh. Meanwhile, the larger and faster Kingbird would skim the tops of the peaks, dropping flares down into the canyon to light the way.

Thirty minutes later, the refueled Kingbird was in the air again, loaded with forty-two flares and enough soft drinks and candy from the snack bar to sustain the hungry crew for what appeared was going to be a long night.

"I'll need plenty of light," Sommer tersely radioed to the Kingbird as they approached the pass. "Direct the light."

Lillegard in the HC-130 Kingbird broke in: "We're passing you— going on ahead of you."

"Wh-what's up?" Sommer stuttered.

Lillegard was thinking of Harbaugh trapped on the black mountain, searching the endless nothingness around him for help. He ordered a signal flare.

"We're going to let him know help's on the way," Lillegard radioed the chopper. "We'll drop a flare near him, then come back and meet you just inside the pass."

Fading in and out of consciousness, Harbaugh brooded. All his life he had done things for himself. Now he felt utterly helpless. Powerless to climb out of the tail of the plane, he rested his head against the fuselage. One hand was covered with a sock. In more hopeful moments, he pushed his arm out between the door and the plane and waved weakly. His face felt stiff, his breathing shallow, his body leaden. Life had become a series of fading dreams.

Perhaps, he thought, if he began at the beginning it might all come back. He remembered a cool, beautiful morning in mid-April and the warmth of a fire he built with his brother, Mark, in the fields in back of his folks' rural Indiana home.

The dream faded. Then there was a voice from the past—his survival-preaching Scoutmaster, who would send teenagers into the woods in winter with a sleeping bag, a candy bar, and one match. The scoutmaster's four words had seared into his brain: "Discover your way back."

Suddenly, as if hallucinating, he saw a spray of incandescence. It burst like an explosion. It was minutes before he understood.

"I'm here," he called weakly. "Hurry."

Minutes later the chopper drummed its way into the black pass, its landing lights like a fluttering candle in the dark tunnel. "Give me lights," Sommer radioed to the HC-130 overhead.

"Get ready for flare one," Lillegard radioed from the Kingbird. Timing was everything, Lillegard knew. He had never commanded a night flare rescue, but he knew the helicopter rescue wouldn't work without plenty of light. The chopper was hovering in a deep bowl flanked by terraces of sheer ice. Without lights, the pilot would be groping in the perilous dark. Any sudden shift in direction, and the helicopter could drift backwards and into the rocks.

For the chopper crew, those first few minutes of descent into the canyon were like hell. Weird shadows darted and shifted, and before the flares started, the inky night was laden with danger. A bitter, icy wind blasted, churned, and roiled the plane like a mini-tornado.

"We're going to drop four-minute flares overlapping every three-and-a-half minutes—got it?" Lillegard radioed down to Sommer.

"Angle 'em," the chopper pilot barked. "Keep 'em out of my rotor blades."

Manning and Johnson, stationed in the rear of the Kingbird next to the open cargo door, began hooking flares to 10-foot taglines. Ten feet away sat loadmaster Brown at the tip end of the plane, legs dangling out into the night.

Manning handed a flare to Johnson, who hooked it to the ring and passed it to Brown, who heaved it out. The tagline popped a cork, disgorging a flare-bearing parachute capable of saturating the area with two million candlepower of light.

Now Lillegard glanced around at his hungry, fatigued crew. They'd been on the job almost twelve hours straight. One airman commented, "We gotta get the guy tonight. Tomorrow he won't need us."

Lillegard, too, was preoccupied with the consequences of tomorrow. As he moved his plane along a narrow perimeter above the peaks and arced flares 4,000 feet downward into the canyon, his thoughts clung to the survivor. He knew the man's fate depended on the determination, skill, and stamina of the aircraft crews.

But deliverance hung on the ocean of light saturating every inch of the search area. Failure of light could bring disaster to the search crews, robbing them of a point of reference in a boundless void.

In the Kingbird cockpit, Lillegard wiped beads of sweat from his forehead. Despite his signal, light failed to issue from the second flare.

"Hey," he yelled, "something's haywire. You take the controls. Fly the turns by my hand signals. I'll synchronize flare drops. Loadmaster—mark, 3, 2, 1—release flare!"

Swiveling his head, Lillegard aimed a bleak look toward the rear of the aircraft. "What the devil's going on back there?" he snarled.

"Duds," Manning replied glumly.

"No!" Lillegard moaned. "The chopper's gotta have light. They're down there flying in a sock. I don't care what you throw out, but dump lights at him fast."

"Roger," replied the loadmaster.

Now the Kingbird was banking for a turn above the narrow part of the pass. Lillegard was stunned by another conjecture. "God," he thought, "what if they're all duds?"

◆

In the chopper below, Sommer was worried. Eyes watering, he babied the controls against the crushing darkness. One minute an encroaching peak was there like a dim phantom, then it was gone, and in moments back again. They were marooned in a booby-trapped sea of darkness.

"How far's the mountain?" he asked anxiously. "Anyone know?"

"About 500 feet last time I saw it," Keller snapped.

"Which direction?"

"Beats me!"

The chopper's radio crackled. "Calling HC-130. Give us light," co-pilot Churchill demanded.

"Got to keep calm," Sommer told himself. "Got to remember where the wall was." The thought of the sheer granite face taunted him and threatened to betray him. Meanwhile a fleeing wraith was sweeping past outside, something he hadn't seen before. "What's that at the right?" he yelled uneasily. "Cliff—or shadow?"

Silence.

Sommer banked the chopper and began inching upward, dreading the possibility of metal biting granite.

"Keep looking, guys," he ordered. "Look hard."

On the freezing earth below, slumped inside the rude shelter, Mike Harbaugh was trembling fiercely. Each breath was agony, each movement a struggle. There was no way now he could move without pain. All he could do was pray: "God—don't let them run out of fuel before they find me." He let his head fall back against the ice-coated mattress and stared into the bleak darkness.

In the Kingbird, Brown, hooked to the plane by a floor strap, lost track of how many flares he had tossed down the canyon. One thing bothered him: The supply was dwindling rapidly.

As the plane banked sharply, Manning and Johnson were thrown toward the open door. Manning grabbed a tie-down strap, Johnson an overhead ring. Blasts of freezing air billowed inside and the plane bounced like a toy. Brown leaned out the ramp, aiming a 2-foot flare like a curveball down into the canyon. The HC-130 pulled along a bend in the pass and started down the other side. Mountain peaks glided by like angry ghosts. Suddenly both navigator and radio operator jumped up, pressing their faces to the cockpit window.

"Look out!" Palmer and Griffin yelled in unison. "Don't turn!"

"We're getting squeezed by peaks," Palmer barked. "Radar's not picking 'em up; gotta climb, gotta go higher."

"Roger," Lillegard rasped, hand-signaling for more altitude. He braced his feet against the floor and ordered himself to think of other things.

For 50 minutes, the HC-130 continued its orbit above the victim on the mountain. Flare after flare exploded in the sky, bringing high noon to the Razors Edge, and drenching the canyon with blinding brilliance.

"Something's terribly wrong," Lillegard yelled. "It's still burning—the same flare."

"It's not the same flare, Captain," Brown replied, "We're tossing them out double."

The air in the cockpit electrified. "You can't do that—we'll run short. Go back to dropping one at a time."

"Roger."

Besides the dwindling flares, the race, Lillegard knew, was now also against the helicopter's fuel supply. He radioed the chopper below: "Hurry up. Locate the guy, or you'll be flying home on fumes." Then the radio crackled again: "Remember, I can't refuel you."

As the chopper tilted at an acute angle, Sommer scanned a slope bathed in eerie brilliance. Something caught his eye: a man's hand that seemed attached to part of the wreckage.

"I see him!" Sommer yelled. "He's still alive! I saw his hand!"

"You sure?" a crewman asked. "Maybe it's a dead man's hand."

"We'll know in a minute," Sommer's mouth was tight, grim.

In the co-pilot's seat Churchill gripped the controls, alarmed. "Go around the pass," he yelled as he saw a flarelike object streaking toward the chopper. "A flare is dropping toward the rotor blades, we're done for. Gotta fly down into the end of the pass and wait it out."

Minutes later the chopper returned, positioning one wheel on a jutting rock extending over a sharp incline 50 feet below Harbaugh's shelter. The flight engineer opened the chopper door and the Arctic winds sliced in like a knife. Beckmann studied the snow under the chopper. How deep was it? Five feet? Twenty-five?

He jumped, landing safely in a chest-deep drift. Gulping air for a few seconds, he strapped on snowshoes and began working his way to the crash site. Beckmann's main worry was Harbaugh's condition. Was he suffering hallucinations? Was he dying? Then a hand moved outside a door at the end of the plane's tailpiece. A voice called: "Here . . . I'm in here."

"Easy," Beckmann said. "What hurts?"

In Harbaugh's punchy state, all he thought of was getting to the helicopter. "Just lift me out . . . get me to the plane."

Harbaugh's bloody face appeared through the flickering light. His nose had been cruelly laid open. His face had become a red ball, his head sagged against the tailpiece.

Beckmann radioed the chopper. "He's alive. Unbelievable! Send a spine board and cervical collar with Keller. We'll have to rip the plane to get him out."

Bending over the tailpiece, Keller and Beckmann yanked away at sheet metal. In the wavering brightness, they strapped Harbaugh to a sleeping bag inside a Stokes Litter, rejecting the sled Keller had brought with him to pull the survivor to a more level place for pickup.

"No time for that," Beckmann barked. "Got to get out of here, fast." Keller pressed his body against the victim, shielding Harbaugh from 100-mph winds as rotor blades thrashed up a blizzard of snow and debris. A chunk of metal ripped into the arm of Beckmann's flight jacket. "Plane part hit me," he called, grabbing a fragment of the fuselage and tossing it out of the way. The para-jumpers strapped Harbaugh tightly into the litter and signaled the chopper with a thumbs-up. Minutes later, Keller and Beckmann stared upward as the stretcher carrying Harbaugh swung like a pendulum outside the chopper door.

"Engineer's having trouble yanking the guy inside the aircraft," Keller shouted. "I'll grab the tagline." Keller pulled on a rope extending to the ground from the stretcher and ran with it down the mountain slope. The lopsided thrust drew the stretcher around crosswise to the cargo door, enabling Proctor to pull the victim inside.

"Nice going," Beckmann called. "Nothing can stop the rescue now."

Only something did.

In the rear of the Kingbird, a popping sound snapped through the engine's roar. Sprawled at the empty cargo ramp, Brown watched something roll and pop less than 8 feet from his legs.

"Flare's going off inside," he yelled. "Get it out!"

Brown knew a two-million-candlepower magnesium flare was nothing to bargain with. Such a flare, once ignited, could melt through flooring and gobble up hydraulic and electrical lines in its path, wiping out the aircraft's power. No extinguisher in the world could put out the blaze.

Just 8 feet of space and scant seconds separated the crew from possible flaming catastrophe.

"Flare's chute's opening. Get it out," Brown's voice screeched into every pair of ear sets on the plane.

The tag ends of the 5-foot-diameter chute attached to the flare now whipped in the swirling wind in the rear of the aircraft, threatening to billow the chute, which would ignite two million candlepower of magnesium. Worse, the gray, cylindrical flare rolled toward 1,000 gallons of highly flammable fuel in the cargo compartment fuel tank a few feet away.

Brown hurtled backwards, landed full length on the floor, hefted his right arm, snatched the canister, and hurled it toward the aft ramp. The flare scooted past Brown's leg, narrowly missing his foot—then cleared the tail of the C-130 and burst into blinding white light before tumbling harmlessly into the night.

Manning and Johnson squinted as the canyon flooded with light like a football field.

The helicopter moved out of Merrill Pass toward Anchorage. Oxygen and IV fluids warmed on the aircraft's air ducts were administered to Harbaugh.

The helicopter now was traveling at "Bingo fuel" (dangerously low). The nearest fueling point was Elmendorf Air Force Base, an impossible hour away.

Trailing the chopper out of the pass, Lillegard contacted Approach Control back in Anchorage: "We're heading along the coast in case of an emergency landing—fuel exhaustion. Flying at 500 feet. Are we clear?"

"Cleared. Do what you have to do," Approach Control replied.

Almost as soon as the helicopter touched down on the Providence Hospital helipad in Anchorage, a team of doctors and nurses trained in cold-weather injuries began ministering to the victim. Harbaugh, who had lost 30 pounds, suffered from a fractured collarbone and ankle, a facial fracture, lacerations of the tongue and nose, and severe frostbite, according to Dr. Michael Eaton.

Doctors had to amputate his left leg below the knee.

But Mike Harbaugh was alive.

Air base rescuers reason that his core temperature was such that he would not have been able to live through another night. They are convinced Harbaugh's fierce determination to live brought him through. Harbaugh recalls that while he was on the mountain, groups from the Pentecostal and the Assembly of God congregations had assembled for Wednesday evening church services and were offering prayers on his behalf in many parts of the United States.

"He had guts," Lillegard said repeatedly while composing his report on the mission. "If I ever meet Mike Harbaugh face-to-face, I will tell him."

The opportunity came six months later at a special ceremony at Elmendorf Air Force Base. Lieutenant Colonel David Hamann, Commander of the 71st Aerospace Rescue & Recovery Squadron, called the chopper and Kingbird crews to the front of the room.

"Gentlemen," he said, "never does our squadron get to talk to people we rescue. I have asked Mike Harbaugh here today so we can meet him. But first he has something to say."

Walking with a cane, awkwardly swinging his artificial limb, Harbaugh faced 100 officers and men of the 71st. He introduced his wife and young son. Then, choked with emotion, he spoke in a room that become absolutely still.

"I really don't know how to thank a squadron of heroes. But my family and I thank you from the bottom of our hearts."

As this story is written, Mike Harbaugh looks forward to his fifth refashioned artificial leg—one that will enable him to run. Each weight gain (he's up to his former 165 pounds) means an expensive new prosthesis fitted to the stump.

Harbaugh survived three days crawling on his stomach in a bear-infested mountain pass. He suffered a shattered ankle and frozen left leg that was later amputated, a broken collarbone, and numerous lacerations. He began hunting a year after his amputation and looks forward to teaching his son to fly some day.

Before his accident, Harbaugh was a short-term locator with Enstar Gas Co., walking several miles a day. But jobs are often scarce for a man with one leg.

Part of his recovery was to keep praying that he would always find work.

Yet each day for Mike on earth is a miracle. "Every day," he says, "is a bonus."

# 16

*Gregory Ysais listened carefully. There was terror in that woman's voice that he couldn't ignore. He ran into the unknown, and arrived in time to save a five-year-old girl from being killed by a California cougar. He received the Carnegie Award for Heroism.*

THE TRACKS were clear. The mountain lion alerted to sounds near the stream. He had trotted out of his lair and crouched at the edge of the bushes, his tail swishing a fan-shaped pattern in the sand. Forty feet away, the Small family—Don, thirty-nine, an optical engineer; his wife, Susan, thirty-seven; and their children, David, nine, and Laura, five—were enjoying their hike in the 7,500-acre Ronald W. Caspers Wilderness Park, 60 miles southeast of Los Angeles in the Santa Ana Mountains.

The big cat returned unnoticed to his hideaway in the dense undergrowth, and Don hiked down the trail with David on that pleasant Palm Sunday afternoon. Susan Mattern-Small and little Laura decided to stay and search the quiet pool in the stream for tadpoles. The pool was 8 to 10 feet deep and 15 to 20 feet across.

Again, the lion alerted—probably to Laura's delighted squeals—and trotted to the edge of the dense clump of bushes. His swishing tail formed another fan-shaped pattern in the sand. Susan and Laura were in the water. Once more, the cat returned to his lair.

The third time the lion came out and made a pattern with its tail, Laura had just stepped out of the water and placed her pail next to her shoes on the sand. Unhurriedly, the cat rose and moved toward Laura. Susan, about 6 feet from her daughter, was looking upstream, but she saw movement out of the corner of her eye and thought it was a trotting dog. Wondering why anyone would let a dog that big run loose, she turned to look and saw the lion with Laura's head in its mouth. In a cat-quick turn, the cougar vanished.

The cat had taken the girl in no more than three seconds, and it took another second for Susan's mind to adjust to the horrible reality. Then she realized that the mountain lion, after entering the bushes, could have gone in any direction on her side of the pool and stream, and that it intended to kill and eat her daughter. Susan screamed in terror.

Don Small heard the screams. For a moment, before recognizing his wife's voice, he thought it was someone joking. Then he raced back down the trail.

"Don," Susan sobbed, "a mountain lion has Laura, and I don't know where it went!"

Don tried to make an instant judgment about which way the lion might have gone. The horrifying truth was that if he was wrong, and if the cougar was leaving the area with Laura, the couple would never see their daughter again. The dense bushes lay between a bluff and the stream. The terrain downstream appeared so steep and rugged that Don thought even a lion wouldn't be able to carry off a child there. He raced upstream, hoping to cut off the animal.

About 200 yards away, perhaps a little farther, Gregory Ysais, a thirty-year-old electronics technician from San Juan Capistrano, also heard the screams. He, too, thought that teenagers were joking. But he stopped and glanced at his wife, Andrea, and his eleven-year-old daughter, Jessica. He listened more carefully. There was real terror in that voice. Greg ran toward the screams, leaving a very frightened wife behind. Was it a gang? A sniper? What was her husband running to? And Andrea couldn't follow, because of Jessica.

Another young couple ran past Andrea; they were yelling, "Get a knife! Get a gun! Get help!" They didn't say why. They had been closer to the stream and had seen Mrs. Small, but they were too intent to stop and tell Andrea what was going on.

Susan Small was in shock. She put on her shoes. She picked up her camera. She wandered aimlessly for a minute, not knowing what else to do. And then Susan heard a moaning call. She ran toward the sound. Laura was in the middle of a dense clump of brush. Susan couldn't get through. She ran around to the other side to find an opening. There was none. Panic-stricken, she ran back. Then she saw the lion. It had Laura by the neck. Susan screamed and screamed and screamed.

Don turned back toward the renewed screams.

Gregory Ysais arrived just as the screams ended. He had no idea why the woman was screaming.

Somehow, Susan made him understand that a lion had dragged her child into those bushes. Greg had hunted as a boy, before urban sprawl had ruined his favorite haunts. He glanced at the bushes and instantly saw the drag-trail through the leaves. He ducked low and crashed through. Yard-high prickly pear cactus blocked him. He tried to jump over the cactus and broke through it with his legs. He landed slightly more than an arm's length from the lion.

The young tom was sitting up, gripping Laura by the neck. The young girl was still squirming and groaning. Greg broke a limb from a dead tree on his left. It wasn't substantial. The lion was in a denlike pocket under the overhanging limbs of the thick brush, so there was no room to swing the limb. Laura's head concealed and screened most of the lion's face. Greg yelled, brandished the limb threateningly, and

CHILD-KILLER CAT

**143**

poked it at the big cat's eyes. The cougar swatted at the limb with one paw. Greg dodged the swats and kept poking at the eyes and yelling. To the lion, Greg must have seemed like a larger animal that was trying to steal his prey. He hung on to Laura's neck and defended himself vigorously with one paw.

Finally, Greg intimidated the cougar so much that it stood up. Perhaps the cat felt cornered in that pocket of underbrush, because he could only move to one side or the other, not back. And perhaps the cat also heard Don Small running toward him through the bushes. The lion started to turn sideways as if to leave with Laura. Greg's yelling and poking became more frantic. In the middle of the turn, probably to defend itself better against Greg, the lion dropped Laura.

Ignoring that the now-unencumbered lion could easily attack him, Greg crowded the cougar, poking at the animal's side. The cat moved a couple of steps sideways, and Ysais jumped between it and Laura. Now he was closer to the cat.

 Greg had no time to think; he could only act. But now the action accelerated so much that, as often happens in such cases, Greg's memory failed to record details. Yet a record of everything that occurred was clearly printed in the sand and soil. Repeatedly, the cougar moved off a step or two, only to whirl back at Ysais threateningly and then skid to a stop just short of an attack.

Greg's eyes never left the lion's. This was not a conscious tactic. It was simply defensive awareness, much like a boxer's. All animals, including predators, know that an unfaltering stare comes from a confident killer about to attack its victim. The cougar must have read more aggression in Greg's eyes than Greg felt. Little by little, the whirling rushes the lion made at Ysais fell shorter and shorter, until Greg had the safety of several feet. He yelled.

Susan's mind had blacked out almost completely when Greg arrived on the scene. She remembers nothing from that moment until he yelled at

DEMONSTRATING how he took the lead from younger brother Justin to "watch for snakes," eight-year-old David Vaught pretends to be on the trail followed by his mother, Kim, and stepfather Chris Brown. Justin's expression is not acting. It's all still very real to him.

TEXAS state predator hunter and trapper Bill McKinney trailed that lion for an entire day with his hounds before treeing it within 100 yards of the attack site. Biologist Doug Waid dispatched it.

TWO weeks before
going after the killer
in a culvert, Florida
nuisance trapper Curtis
Lucas survived a tussle
with an 11-foot alligator
that bit five holes in his
aluminum boot.

JACK KILPATRIC is arguably the
first, perhaps only, man ever to punch
a lion to save a hound—three times!—
and survive the ordeal.

WILDLY turbulent 50-knot winds whipping over and around mountaintops hurled Jim Munson's Caribou straight up, straight down, tail first, and upside down, and then a wind shear pancaked it on the only place flat enough to keep it from rolling down the mountain.

CAUGHT by a sudden storm, Roger and Pat Stewart had only one space blanket for shelter. Going into hypothermia, Roger pulled Pat out into the rain and hail to dance and sing gospel songs to raise their body temperatures. That began the worst five days of their lives.

THE tragic death of 18-year-old newlywed Adeana Dickison was the powerful catalyst motivating the Alaska Mat-Su Borough Dive Team's determination to find a way to save anybody, anywhere, from the 500-pound grip of glacial silt on Alaska's dangerous "mud flats."

KNOWING he'd go into shock and die before being found, outdoorsman Donald Wyman not only cut off his leg, but calmly guided his rescue, even refusing a sedative for fear of becoming unconscious and somebody else getting excited and making a mistake.

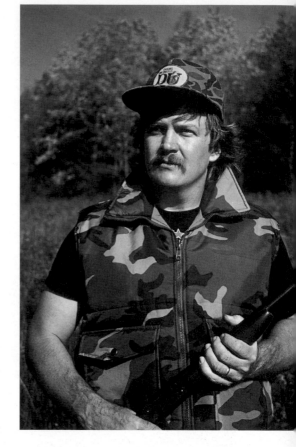

SNOWED in at cougar camp for a month and barely surviving on flour and beans, Steve Matthes dared to try lion steak and declared it the best meat he ever ate. (I have eaten it, too, and agree. Adventurers should never waste lion meat. —LM)

TWO weeks before going after the killer in a culvert, Florida nuisance trapper Captain Thorne Tasker at the wheel. He showed superhuman strength while untangling the rescue helicopter's weights on the drop line, then couldn't push the button to open a car door with his left thumb. Only then did he remember breaking that thumb a couple of days earlier.

THE catwalk above the wheelhouse is where Captain Tasker hung by his left ankle (hooked behind the railing's corner post) with only his left hand gripping the mast support/radio ground at a 60-degree angle while the *Nowitna* rolled violently.

THE second time the dogs and boar fought in the water, a blue Lacey stock dog was nearly drowned.

NEARING the beach, Barefoot Bob grabbed the hind legs and wheelbarrowed the boar ashore.

THE boar, now walleyed and mad about everything it experienced that day.

JOHN WEILAND, with a crushed ankle and two leg bones broken, lowered himself down a 20-foot vertical icefall with two ice axes, then painfully dragged himself down a 45-degree crusted snow field by preventing an uncontrollable slide with the axes. At the river, he signaled a passerby for help.

BRIAN TEALE was pinned under a crushing weight of ice with broken bones and a punctured lung. He would die unless help could be found quickly.

SYNERGISTIC survivors Gary and Dorothy Franklin are among the rare 10 percent of couples whose marriages don't fail during the horrors of fire, medical treatment, and psychological recovery of a burn victim.

THIS is the cave where Byron Glacier's ice melt emerges. (Photo courtesy of Thomas Shemanske.)

BYRON GLACIER. Just left of dead center is the cave outlet for the ice melt where Glacier Girl would have fallen onto boulders had the crevasse not caught her first. (Photo courtesy of Mary Hopson.)

her, but these words are clearly burned in her memory: "Pick up your baby and get out of here!"

Mrs. Small ran through the cactus and grabbed little Laura. The child looked dead. She wasn't struggling anymore. Her scalp was in shreds, and her head was covered with blood from fifty cuts and punctures in her face and head.

At that instant, Don Small came crashing through the bushes, and the lion gave up. He couldn't defend his kill against three humans. "Get her to the clearing," Greg yelled as the cougar ran into the bushes.

Greg ran ahead, but the Smalls didn't stop at the clearing. If there were any life left in Laura, only fast action could save her. They ran to a dirt road and then toward the nearest road open to vehicles. At first Susan carried the girl, then Don, and both continuously cried out for others to get help. "There's a mountain lion," they called. The park was crowded with 250 people that day.

Greg also encountered other people who offered to run ahead. Exhausted and slowing down, he let them do it.

One man came back to meet the Smalls and carried Laura the last 100 yards to the road, where a ranger truck was already waiting. At the visitor center, they learned that although the regional trauma center was just 20 minutes away by ambulance, there was a rodeo at San Juan Capistrano. They could easily become entangled in traffic. A helicopter could get them to Mission Community Hospital in Mission Viejo in only three minutes, but no helicopters were available.

Finally, an Orange County Sheriff's Department helicopter was brought in. Laura's parents followed in a police car.

In the helicopter, Laura regained consciousness enough to ask whether her mother and father were safe. Hearing her mother's screams had made her fear that something had happened to them, too. This occurred about an hour after the 1:20 P.M. attack.

By 5:30, Laura was in surgery, where doctors worked for thirteen hours. Besides the deep lacerations, there were five punctures through

Laura's skull, and one half of the circumference of her right eye was damaged. A bone fragment lodged against her brain paralyzed her right side.

Joel Shows, a Louisiana-born federal trapper with almost twenty years of experience, was called from his home near San Bernardino to help catch the lion. In addition to his job with the U.S. Fish and Wildlife Service (he was later transferred to the U.S. Department of Agriculture), Shows maintains a pack of his own strain of treeing Walker hounds, which he uses to sport-hunt bobcats. Although there hadn't been an open season on lions in California since 1972, Joel was occasionally asked to use his hounds to kill a cougar on a state depredation permit.

Shows arrived at 9:30 P.M. The tracks were so clear that it was like standing there watching it happen," Joel said. "When I saw those three places where the lion had lain swishing its tail, I thought at first that there was a bunch of lions. Then I realized that the same cat had made all of the signs and tracks. I was terribly afraid that the little girl wouldn't live. There was a big circle of blood, soaked 1½ inches into the sand in the place where the lion had dragged her. Blood had splattered up onto the leaves of the bushes. It got up there when the lion shook her as a dog shakes a rabbit."

Joel tried to start his hounds on the lion's trail, but they couldn't smell it anywhere except in that pocket in the brush.

The lion had returned shortly after Ysais drove him off. Not long after the attack, a man with a gun (illegal in the park) was seen pointing it into the bushes. He said, "A lion went in there. It was drinking from the stream. It walked right past me."

That prompted the dispatch of a helicopter to search the area for the lion. The circling helicopter probably drove the cat into another part of its territory.

"We tried until 2 A.M. to get the hounds on a track," Joel said, "but too many people had left scent around the area. By the time we left, the people, including myself, and my eight hounds had obliterated nearly all of the tracks."

Early the next morning, Shows joined men from the Orange County Park Service, Orange County Animal Control, and the California Department of Fish and Game to resume the hunt. Before the attack, park rangers had been seeing numerous lion tracks on the big ridge above the attack site. Assuming that the lion had moved into that part of his home territory, the hunters decided to free the hounds there. No fresh tracks were found, however. Joel twice stopped his hounds from running bobcats, but nothing promising occurred until two animal-control men delivered a rumor that a lion had been seen crossing the lower road.

Joel asked where and took his hounds for a look, but found no tracks. This brought him close to the attack site, however, so he decided to have another look. Sure enough, the lion had returned. Tracks matching those under the bushes were freshly printed right where the lion had grabbed little Laura.

It was then 7:30 A.M. The tracks were not very fresh, and the hounds couldn't carry the trail, but Shows wasn't worried. His hounds drifted along a cold track instead of following it print by print. One hound will bark its discovery of a slight scent, and then the others will race in to help. If they can't track, they fan out again until another hound smells something. In this way, the hounds can roll along rapidly on a very cold trail. The lion's scent led the pack around the basin, in and out of the canyon, and up and down the ridge.

Hounds quickly get out of hearing in canyons and behind ridges, so Joel was driven around to the top of the mountain, where he could hear the chase better. An hour later, Shows heard his pack barking, and rushed down to the dogs. The lion was in a tree, but Shows was unarmed and couldn't kill it. Anyway, the decision had been made to tranquilize the cougar, not with the intention of releasing a killer cat in another area, but so that it could be studied alive in an effort to learn why it had attacked.

As Joel Shows called for someone to bring the tranquilizer gun, the lion exhibited no signs of nervousness. Normally, too much yelling will make a cougar jump out of a tree. The cat showed fear only when the dogs moved.

Captain Rod Shackelford of the Department of Fish and Game heard Joel and the hounds, but it took another hour before he could round up the necessary men and equipment. The cat remained calm.

Finally, one of the animal-control people loaded the tranquilizer gun, and Joel tied back his hounds so they would be safely out of the cat's reach. A warden shot the animal in the shoulder. The cougar bit at the dart but couldn't reach it. Then the cat bailed out of the tree, jumped up another, dropped out of that one, and went up a third. There the tom lost his footing, fell, and vanished in the bushes.

Joel had been told that the lion would be unconscious in five minutes. He waited six minutes before releasing his hounds to find the animal. By the time the hounds had lined out on the track, eight to ten minutes had elapsed.

The chase led out of the canyon, over a ridge, and across a big brushy flat. Joel ran behind the pack as hard as he could go, knowing that a properly tranquilized lion shouldn't be traveling that far.

Shows heard his hounds catch the lion. The cougar roared as loudly as the dogs barked. When Shows caught up, they were fighting in thick brush. The cat's hindquarters would go out from under him when he tried to whirl around at a dog attacking his rear. Otherwise, the cougar gave no indication of being tranquilized. His forward moves were normal. The hounds were getting braver and braver now that Shows had arrived.

That's when Joel realized that, for a second time, he had run off unarmed and left everyone else behind. Joel yelled for someone with a gun. No one answered. Still yelling, Joel looked for a club. He was afraid that if he didn't do something soon, he would hear the dreadful cry of a dying hound. Ordinarily, arthritis in his fingers makes it impossible for

Joel to break a pencil, but somehow he broke off a green limb. He started wading into the bushes just as one of the wardens answered his calls.

Joel shouted: "You got a gun?"

"Yes!"

Shows dropped his club and ran to meet the warden, who handed him what he wanted least: the tranquilizer gun that had underdosed the lion.

"Oh, hell! That cat will kill some of my dogs!" he shouted.

"Well, I've got a pistol, too," the warden said.

Joel took the .38 Special revolver and forced his way through the almost impenetrable bushes to within arm's reach of the lion. Straight down was the only way to shoot without hitting a hound. Shows stuck out his arm, pointed the barrel down, and fired. The sound of the .38 made the hounds all the braver, but the lion, although struck in the shoulder, gave no signs of being hit. Quickly, Joel fired again, and the cougar dropped instantly with a broken neck.

The lion was a young tom, eighteen to twenty-four months old, and weighed 92 pounds. He was thin, but only in that way that young animals are before they fill out. An autopsy revealed no health problems that would have forced him to seek easier prey. In addition, Joel Shows found two deer kills in the animal's territory, so it couldn't have been lack of food that had led him to attack a human being. Nor was the cougar a released pet that had lost its fear of humans. He had not been declawed or defanged. He had none of the tooth decay usually found in pet lions.

Concern arose over whether the right lion had been killed, because no human hair was found in the intestines. But little Laura did not actually lose any of her scalp, even though it was badly shredded. The tracks at the attack site matched the cougar's paws in size. And behavior is an even better indicator of an animal's identity. The cat had returned to the attack site and to his lair, where the chase had begun, and until the very end he had demonstrated his lack of fear of humans, as do many animals that live in parks and other places where hunting has been forbidden for a long time. Sport hunting can be used to teach many animals, including mountain lions, to fear human beings and to stay away from them.

At the time of this writing, little Laura Small is at home with her parents. Her ability to speak is returning. Her control over her right side is slowly improving, but it's uncertain whether she will ever have full use of her arm and hand again. After four operations, she still has almost no sight in her injured eye.

Susan Small is both grateful and bitter—grateful because Laura is alive, and bitter because she believes that the incident never should have happened.

"Right now," Susan told me with a sad smile, "Laura is experiencing the 'princess syndrome.' How can you get angry at a poor little girl who's been attacked by a lion? But her real personality is unchanged, and she's alive. And more and more I understand what Gregory Ysais did for us."

Susan Small's mood changes sharply, however, when she reflects on how the lion showed no fear of humans. She blames that, in part, on California's fourteen-year moratorium on lion hunting.

"When you put your finger on one part of a situation," she said, "you'd better have a good sense of what will happen to the rest of it. The governor refused to continue the moratorium on hunting cougars, but even so, the California Department of Fish and Game is insisting on more study before opening a season on lions."

Two days after killing the Caspers Park lion, Joel Shows was called in to hunt another cougar that had attacked a dog in Idyllwild, California, and that was suspected of killing two others and injuring one more. The lion had walked alongside the house and leaped at the dog on an outside flight of stairs. When it missed, the cat sank its fangs and claws into a step, and then bounded to the top of the stairs, where it slammed into the door just as it caught the 80-pound Pit Bull/German Shepherd cross. The homeowner opened the door and saw the cat.

Show's hounds treed the lion on a boulder 300 yards from the house. The cat had taken the partially eaten dog to the boulder.

"The frightening part about this," Joel Shows said, "is the number of children playing in the area. One boy, looking down at the rock where I killed the lion, said, 'We were playing down there just yesterday!' If this keeps up, someone is going to be killed, and you can bet it's going to be a child."

# 17

*A famous line in Tennessee Williams's play* Cat on a Hot Tin Roof *reads, "I must rely on the kindness of strangers." So it was here. Fortunately, this time one of the strangers was a trained survivor.*

TRAINED Air Force para-rescueman Staff Sergeant Eric Sachs, with forty-two rescues to his credit, wasn't thinking about saving anybody on his day off. He'd left his climbing gear at home in his wife Lynn's car. He and Lynn were in his own car, driving out to the vicinity of Byron Glacier because she wanted something from the visitor center in the draw between Byron and Portage Glaciers. Once there, however, they decided to hike the mile or less up the trail for a closer look at Byron Glacier. Along the way, they passed a husband, wife, and kids with skis sticking out of their backpacks.

"Did you see that, Lynn? There's no snow down here, and higher up the glacier that snowfield is hard and slick from thawing and freezing. Skis have no grip on it. They just slip and slide. The skier has no control. That's dangerous."

Eric and Lynn hiked to the end of Byron for a look at the cave where glacier melt flows out from under the ice, then walked on to see what the other people in the area were doing. They passed a young man with skis, accompanied by a young woman carrying a camera and wearing sneakers. Tourists, Eric thought, as he and Lynn hiked a short way onto the ice to a safe place where he could keep an eye on their dog. Fairly close was a large crevasse across the toe of the glacier, varying from 6 to 10 feet across, then narrowing and finally closing to a fault line as it went up the slope. People were slipping and sliding near the fault line. A fall could send someone careening down the slope and into the crevasse.

The young man who had been with the girl and another man hiked past and started up the glacier without crampons on their feet. "You watch, Lynn. Somebody is going to get hurt real bad, and I'm going to have a rescue mission before we leave here."

The girl came along behind the men. As she neared, Lynn looked at her feet and said, "Boy! Are you hiking up there in sneakers? It's pretty slippery up there."

"Oh, it's not that bad," the girl answered. "There's pretty good traction."

Survivors are risk-takers, but history is littered with stories of people who died when they let overconfidence in their own capabilities overcome prudent common sense. In the end, they either perish or have to be rescued by those who, over time, did work on advancing their survival skills. Although she would prove to be quite intelligent, the girl in this story was too full of herself to use good judgment. To avoid embarrassing her with her lack of survivor traits, we'll just call her Glacier Girl.

One of the things she apparently hadn't learned is that there are sun cups in the surface of glaciers that can make going up the slope similar to treading on steps. Going down is a different matter. When a heel that's not outfitted with a crampon makes contact with the cup's curve, the foot slides away and the person falls.

The next time Eric looked, Glacier Girl was 150 feet up the 20-degree slope and right in the fault line with the crevasse. She was taking pictures, and just as she turned to shoot in another direction, she fell and started to slide. At first Eric thought she was sliding intentionally, but then he saw her eyes become huge with fear. "Help her! Help her!" Lynn yelled.

Glacier Girl was screaming in fright. Her body began a slow spin as she streaked toward the crevasse. She saw Eric and yelled, "Stop me!" His natural instincts were to try, but it happened too fast, which was a stroke of good luck. Had he been able to grab an arm or leg, Glacier Girl's momentum would have dragged him along with her. It is not wise for a person trained in rescue work to place himself in the same predicament as the victim. Feeling terribly helpless, Eric watched as she flew into the narrow V crack and heard the slap-slap-slap of her body bouncing from wall to wall as she fell.

Panic was spreading among the bystanders. "Lynn, let's get you off the glacier," Eric said. "I don't want you to get hurt. Then I'll go see what can be done."

As he walked toward a fellow peering into the crevasse, he called out, "Anybody have climbing gear or a rope?" Nobody responded. But the fellow at the crevasse was talking with the girl. They seemed to know each other.

"Can you see her down there?"

"Yeah."

"How far down is she?"

"About 30 feet."

Eric crawled to the edge and could see her wedged in the bottom by her chest with her right side down, her head turned to the right and facing down. Her right arm dangled below her, and the left seemed wedged in awkwardly by her head, perhaps broken. She was angled down, with her feet and legs slightly higher than her head. The lip of the crevasse wall she fell over was about 5 feet higher than the lip of the opposite wall. Her chest was against the higher wall and her back against the lower.

Some of the onlookers worried that her body heat would melt the ice and she would slide deeper, perhaps into the river of melted ice below the glacier. On the other hand, the ice would lower her body temperature. And Glacier Girl was lightly dressed, adding to the urgency. She had to be rescued quickly, before she reached late-stage hypothermia. For Eric, what really made every minute count was the ringing sound of moving ice he had heard. Depending on how it moves, a crevasse can open and close in days, even hours.

Eric sent a bystander to the visitor center to get rescue gear, at least a rope, and medical supplies. Two minutes later, he realized that the man probably wouldn't know the right things to ask for, so he'd better go himself. "Keep talking to reassure her and keep her mind off her situation," Eric told the friend, then ran with her boyfriend to his van to speed up the last quarter-mile to the center.

Glacier Girl was in no mood for light conversation. Her reaction to the friend's first question was silence. When he asked how long she had known her boyfriend, she reluctantly answered, "Seven years." Then she shut down the conversation by saying, "My head hurts. It's bleeding."

At the center, Eric learned that the bystander he sent had already been there. The state troopers had been notified, and were assembling a volunteer rescue team out of Girdwood. The visitor center itself had nothing at all—not even a rope—to help rescue an accident victim.

When a trooper drove up, Eric got in the car, identified himself as a trained para-rescueman with the 71st, gave him the details of the accident, and, most important, explained what equipment he would need to get the girl out of the crevasse. He hoped the trooper would call the rescue team and tell them what gear was needed, so time wouldn't be wasted on a second trip. Darkness was approaching.

"They're organizing a team at Girdwood," the officer replied. "We'll just have to wait."

In the meantime, Mike Miller and Marko and Vicki Radonich were coming off the glacier after a day of ice climbing. Someone noticed their climbing gear and shouted to them that a girl was wedged in a crevasse. Mike, an oil-drilling foreman for BP, had just taken a course in emergency trauma treatment. He had a seat harness, ice screws to fasten into the rim above the girl, and 165 feet of rope to thread through both seat and ice screws, so he could lower himself.

About halfway down, his six-foot-one, 178-pound frame could go no lower. He was just too big. But he could see that the girl was seriously threatened by frostbite and hypothermia. Mike tied a carabiner, a strong oval-shaped clip, to the end of his rope and lowered it through the little gap at the small of her back and down to her right hand. She wasn't capable of enough movement to attach it to her jeans or jacket to be pulled out. "Try holding onto the carabiner with both hands," Mike suggested. She tried, which showed that at least her left arm wasn't broken. But each time Mike pulled, she couldn't hang on. She didn't have enough strength.

About that time, Eric arrived. The Girdwood crew was only minutes behind. They had no climbing gear, but they did have another rope and medical supplies. Seeing that Mike couldn't get low enough, Eric knew that his five-foot-eight, 150-pound body could at least get closer. Vicki Radonich loaned him her seat harness, ice screws, and rope. As Mike went up for more rope, the volunteers lowered Eric headfirst. When he was a few feet above her, holding a rope with a slipknot at the end, Eric said, "Point your feet out." She pointed the left foot, but in the gathering darkness Eric couldn't see the right foot at all. One foot would have to do. He slid the noose over her foot, drew it snug, and asked the volunteers to lift him up out of the way, so they could pull her free.

A discussion now developed. Someone cautioned that they might pull her leg out of joint. Before they could arrive at a consensus, Glacier Girl barked, "Get your act together up there and get me out."

Finally, she heard the rescuers call. "Get ready." The rope snugged up and pulled, and she screamed, "My head! Stop! You're hurting me!"

Minutes went by until another plan was formed. Eric said, "I'm coming back down. I'm going to drop a noose right in front of your head. You'll have to get both wrists into it, then I'll pull it snug."

This plan would reduce the pressure on her leg, and when her right arm was pulled up it would free her head, which had been stuck between the walls. In reality, the plan did do these things, but her body was still jammed in.

Eric then told the two crews to get farther apart so they could pull her back and forth. The method would be like pulling first at one side and then at the other side of a cork to remove it from a bottle. There would be no hard yanking, just gentle back-and-forth pressure. Eric told the girl to exhale all of the air from her lungs to make her chest as small as possible, then shouted "Go!" to the first team. After less than a minute of seesaw pulling, he could happily proclaim, "She's moving! Pull her up."

A helicopter flew her to Providence Hospital in Anchorage, where she was treated for a concussion, hypothermia, bruises, and lacerations.

Mike Miller was probably the only person to find a silver lining in this incident. If the crevasse had not been there to catch the girl, chances were great that her slide would have continued on to the end of the glacier and the cave, where she would have fallen about 15 feet into shallow ice water that flowed over a bed of rocks. That would have been far more damaging than bouncing down the walls of an ice vise.

Eric Sachs was reprimanded for performing an off-duty rescue.

In the aftermath, the ungrateful Glacier Girl thought that she'd been responsible for getting herself out of her mess, claiming that she'd personally directed the rescuers.

# 18

*A ten-month challenge like the one in this story may be way beyond the call of duty, but survive it this hunter did, despite all the odds against him—some of his own making, and some beyond his control.*

THE LEDGE threading across the face of the cliff had become so narrow that Steve Coy couldn't bring one leg around the other to take a step. The ledge was no longer level, either. It sloped downward. He scooted his right foot forward, feeling for solid footing, not daring to look down. He had looked once and nearly froze at the sight of the treetops hundreds of feet below. His boot seemed to be gripping, so he hugged the cliff and dragged his left foot up behind the right.

Raised in Springfield, Illinois, where it would be easy to imagine that the entire world is flat, Steve didn't even like to watch mountain climbing on TV. But what concerned him most at this moment was that he wasn't wearing appropriate mountain boots, with Vibram soles. Instead he was wearing insulated rubber boots designed more for mud than rock.

Steve knew it was a mistake to be on this ledge, of course. And it wasn't the first mistake he had made that day. But it was too late to worry, and there was no time for regrets. A bighorn sheep that he had wounded was somewhere ahead of him on this ledge. He had a responsibility to fulfill, and was determined to carry it out.

Hunting this ram—the entire hunt, in fact—had been a cliffhanger from the very start. In Wyoming, sheep permits are distributed by means of a lottery-type luck of the draw. Steve had applied four years in a row before his name was selected. He applauded his luck—until, that is, he got to the ledge. He hunted the Absaroka Mountains of the Shoshone National Forest in northwestern Wyoming for most of the two-month season without seeing a ram with a legal three-quarters curl. Finally he caught a fleeting glimpse of a band of five good rams on a dead run across the head of a canyon. There was no sense following. It was almost dusk, and they had seen him first. He returned the next day instead.

Early in the day, he and brother Walt climbed the Ishawooa Mesa trail on horseback. At daybreak, they began glassing the cliffs, canyons, and grassy meadows of the large ridge. It was October 29, and the season would end on October 31. Steve was getting nervous about how little time they had left. Once you have drawn a permit in Wyoming, you're not eligible to apply again for another five years. Add five years for unpredictable lottery luck, and it's easy to see that a Wyoming bighorn sheep permit can be a once-in-a-lifetime affair. Steve didn't want his one opportunity to end in failure.

At last, about 2 p.m., he peered over a ledge into a huge rocky bowl and spotted a young ram 200 yards below. His blood rushed while he continued glassing, looking for a legal ram. Suddenly, there one was, bedded down on the lower side of a massive chimney rock. His brown coat had blended perfectly with the rocks, making him difficult to see.

All that remained now was to place his shot. Steve forced himself to calm down. His perhaps once-in-a-lifetime hunt was reaching its finale.

The ram was facing away at a slight angle. Steve was looking down at his back, wondering where to place the bullet, where it would come out, what the range was, how much the bullet would drop, and how much he should compensate for shooting mostly straight down.

For a full 30 minutes, he and Walt quietly sized up the ram and planned the shot. When Steve squeezed off the round, both sheep vanished behind the chimney rock. He felt confident that the shot was well-placed, but just to be sure, Walt remained above to act as spotter. He would yell if he saw the ram move.

Steve worked his way down slide rock, timber and patches of snow. It was slow going after what must have been a half hour after the shot—plenty of time for a badly wounded animal to stiffen up—Steve found a trail of blood where the ram had bolted from it's bed. The dead big horn had to be nearby.

"Walt," he yelled in relief, "Blood!"

Rocks clattered in a shallow draw just 30 yards below. The ram! Perhaps not hit as hard as hoped. Obviously, it hadn't stiffened and was now moving. Yelling had been a serious mistake. Quietly following the blood trail, would have been the better course of action.

Steve hurried into the draw, caught sight of the ram, shot and missed. The ram vanished through the trees. Then he reappeared walking broadside across another little draw. Again, he shot and missed. Suddenly, it lay down in plain sight of Steve. Yet another miss. About then, Steve discovered that the rear mount of his new scope had loosened, perhaps when he fell on the way down. Two cartridges were left.

Steve followed the ram downhill, thinking that he was "walking him home" toward the rigs parked far below near the south fork of the Shoshone River. Slowly, however, it dawned on Steve that this animal had an escape plan. The ram turned left around some large rocks and headed across the slope toward a stand of conifers. He was just inside the trees going straight away when he stopped and gazed to his right—completely unaware of Steve's presence only 30 yards behind him. With the scope loose, Steve pointed the rifle and hoped. The rifle roared, and the ram collapsed like a dynamited building.

Steve was elated to at last have a fine trophy head and meat for the freezer. Looking up toward Walt, Steve cut loose with a victory whoop that echoed all over the canyon. When he turned back to the ram—no victory. It was gone.

The trees ended at the beginning of a ledge across the face of the cliff. The ram could have gone nowhere else, so Steve followed.

At first, the ledge was decently wide and flat, but it narrowed to a dead-end rock abutment. Growing from below the abutment, and leaning away from the cliff at a 30-degree angle, was a pine tree about 18 inches in diameter. It was only 6 inches from the ledge, so the sheep must have somehow climbed the rock. Sheep can do remarkable things with hooves that have clefts and hard edges that grip and soft almost adhesive inner pads that cling. Steve couldn't do that climb.

There was only one way to go on. Steve weighed the idea against a failed hunt and was sorely tempted to quit. But a hunter has a responsibility to do everything in his power to recover a wounded animal. He wrapped his arms around the tree and bellied around the trunk with his backside hanging over the cliff.

Conditions only got worse. The ledge became so narrow that he had to scoot along, and it's slope threatened to slide Steve off into oblivion.

Again, he considered quitting. Another rock, probably 6½ feet tall, jutted out from the cliff and blocked the ledge. Beyond the rock, the cliff face curved out to the right, allowing Steve to see the ledge. It tapered off to nothing, so the assumption was that the sheep must have fallen. Or he could be out of sight just beyond the rock. Yes! There was blood on the rock.

A tiny dent in the rock gave Steve a toehold to hoist head, shoulders, and gun over the top. He clung there by the weight of his belly and chest against the rock and stared into the face of the surprised sheep. The ram stood up not 10 feet away. Steve pointed the rifle and pulled the trigger on his last cartridge.

The sheep disappeared from the ledge. Moments later a thud came from far below, then two more thuds. With compact binoculars Steve spotted the dead ram 500 feet below.

There was no way down the cliff to the ram, so Steve slowly edged his way back off the ledge and began to climb back up to Walt. It was grueling. The fine scree that he had easily slid down was now making him slip backward one step for most of the steps he took forward. Nearby, bighorn ewes stared at him as he moved, apparently unintimidated because of his near-helplessness and lack of maneuverability.

Two hours later, he made it to the ridgetop trail, exhausted. The daylight was all but gone. But worse, Steve found that the consequences of his premature victory whoop were not yet concluded. Walt was gone. He had taken Steve's yell to mean that he had the ram and would continue on down to the rigs. Walt got the horses and rode down to wait.

Steve started down the trail, but daylight was slipping quickly away. The edge of a snow front was moving in. Temperatures were dropping rapidly. He hurried to gather enough firewood before complete darkness fell. It had been a sunny, rather balmy day with low humidity and temperatures in the 50s. He was wearing only blue jeans, a denim jacket with a light polyester vest beneath, and a cowboy hat. With his back to a tree to break some of the wind, he built a fire in a ring of rocks, almost in his lap.

In the meantime, Walt was near panic from worrying. At midnight, he drove out to a phone. Tired and confused, Walt was without words to express his fears when Steve's wife, Connie, answered. "Where's Steve?" Walt blurted. It's hard to grasp what effect those two words can have on a just-awakened woman in the middle of the night, but Connie had the presence of mind to call the couple's pastor. He convinced her that Steve was level-headed, and would do the correct things to make it through the night.

Walt wasn't quite that sure. He feared Steve could have fallen off a cliff. He returned to the site with a friend, plus some search-and-rescue people. They glassed the mountain for a fire, saw none, and suspected that Steve was already dead. There was nothing they could do except wait for daylight.

◆

For one anxious moment that night, Steve's own confidence wavered as well. The wind was terribly cold and snow was starting to fall. He was becoming damp, and so was the wood he depended upon for survival.

Around 2 A.M. Steve heard grunting in the timber below him. He was working as a staff biologist for the Cody Resource Area Office, Bureau of Land Management, at the time and was aware that there had been at least three different sightings of anywhere from one to three grizzlies in the vicinity. He threw more wood on the fire. The rifle was empty.

Few things have been as welcome to anybody as the first crack of dawn was to him that morning. He hadn't slept a wink. Steve was stiff from leaning against the tree. His backside felt nearly frozen, and his front was cherry red from the fire. He immediately put out the fire and started down the mountain. As Steve broke into the sage foothills one-and-a-half hours later, Walt and two search-and-rescue people were approaching on horseback. A red plane soared low as one of the horsemen radioed the pilot to abort the mission. Steve had been sighted.

Walt tried to apologize for leaving that night, but staying wouldn't have helped. He couldn't have gotten back up the mountain to Steve in the dark. Going for professional search-and-rescue help was the right decision.

Steve went home and spent the rest of the day getting warm and resting in bed. The shivers and shakes had continued all night, and although he felt no mental confusion, he had surely been on the verge of hypothermia.

Walt and a friend hiked into the cliffs that day, but they couldn't reach the ram.

The following morning Steve joined them in trying to come up from below the ram on horseback. He was able to identify where the bighorn was by the box canyon it lay above. As they glassed the area they could see ravens, magpies, and an eagle dining on Steve's kill. They were within 120 feet, but it was straight up a vertical rock wall.

On Sunday, a young mountain climber volunteered to scale the cliff. Steve was "belaying"—hanging onto the rope as the climber ascended, to catch him if he fell. Steve was relieved when the climber gave up, exhausted.

Steve returned to work on Monday, and by Tuesday morning, two more climbers offered to go up the mountain and try to salvage his ram. They started too late, and it was more than they had bargained for. At 80 feet up, and within 40 feet of Steve's sheep, they had to call it quits in the waning daylight.

All hopes of salvaging any edible meat were now gone, but Steve couldn't get the sheep out of his mind. He didn't kill the animal just to see it die. It seemed dishonorable to let the whole animal rot away into nothing.

A helicopter pilot offered to solve his problem.

"I'm flying up the South Fork every day, anyway," the pilot said. "In a couple minutes, I could drop you in, you could pick up the horns, and we could be gone."

Steve was elated. But not for long. The pilot's commonsense solution bogged down in bureaucratic nitpicking. Was the ram possibly located a few feet over the imaginary (and inaccurate) "wilderness" line that the pilots were supposed to avoid? Would the pilot's supervisor authorize such a two-minute pause? Would the supervisor talk to his supervisor? The bureaucratic chain of command being harder to scale than the 120-foot cliff, Steve gave up the idea.

Three times Steve drove 25 miles up the south fork of the Shoshone River to sit and look at the cliffs where his ram lay. Once, Connie went along. Seeing the terrain did not help her understand Steve's tenacity. In fact, her concern and determination to keep him away from the cliffs became almost as strong as his own determination to retrieve those horns.

In March, Mark De Forneaux, one of the climbers who got within 40 feet of the ram, offered to try again. This time it would be with ice climbing equipment. Unfortunately, an early spring thaw had made the ice unstable.

By summer, Cody pilot Ed Christensen suggested that Steve and he fly over to Mesa, shoot pictures, then study them to think up a plan of attack. No new routes of access were apparent from the air, but for weeks Steve pored over photographs and topography maps looking for a clue. One possibility suggested itself. They could approach the opposite end of the cliff with the ledge on horseback, and then they'd be very near the site where the ram fell. What lay between that approach and the sheep was anybody's guess.

Lee Gaskill, Jake Woobert, and Loren Bales agreed to explore the possibility. Loren provided the horses and stock truck. They drove up to Mesa and discovered Steve's little rock-rimmed fire circle sitting right in the trail. Loren stepped off and kicked it out of the way. Steve felt strange about that. That was the site of a life-and-death experience for him. The rocks were like a monument. Part of Steve was thinking that Loren should have asked first, while another part was chuckling that Loren had booted his historical marker out of the way so that his horses could pass.

After tying off the horses, the men descended to the rim of a canyon that overlooked the kill site. The carcass was below them on the opposite side of the canyon. Again, they took pictures so they could figure out a plan of descent. As Steve looked across the canyon cliff, he could see no trace of the ledge where he had followed the sheep. He broke out in a clammy sweat and began to understand Connie's strong opposition every time he returned to the Mesa.

Two weeks later, the four men were back with two 25-foot rope-and-wood ladders, two 25-foot aluminum-chain ladders, and all the ropes of various sizes and lengths that they could scrounge. Steve resolved that this would be his last try. He couldn't ask any more of either his friends or Connie.

They tied the horses and descended a steep watershed to a 60-degree slope in the rock above a hole of unknown depth. It wasn't a fully 360-degree hole, but the rim circled around for more than 180 degrees. Below the edge, the rock cut back, creating an overhang that prevented them from seeing the bottom.

They tied two ladders in tandem, secured one end to a boulder, and dropped the other down the 60-degree slope and over the edge. It hung in midair, making no noises to suggest it had made contact with the bottom. They pulled it up and added a third length. Again, they heard no signs of contact with the bottom.

Temperatures began to fall. A front was moving in, and rain began to drizzle. The rocks felt slick. Steve was on the verge of giving up once again. The ladders had never been tested, and he had no intention of adding a fourth. Suddenly, someone moved the ladder and yelled, "Hey, I think we hit bottom."

One of the fellows immediately tied a safety rope to his waist and started down the ladder. He hesitated on the last rung before the ladder dropped over the edge into mid-air. Ten minutes later, despite the urging and encouragement of the others, he crawled back up and removed the safety rope. The expressions on the faces of the other men told Steve the unspoken message: "It's your sheep; you go get it."

He hesitated. He didn't want to dangle on a rope ladder. But this was his last chance to finish a hunt that had now gone on for ten months. "Okay," Steve finally said, making his excuses in advance, "but we'll just have to see whether I go over the edge or come back up like he did."

With a pack on his back and rope wound all over him, he forced himself to go over the edge onto that swaying ladder. Carefully, slowly, he climbed down with white-knuckle grips that didn't relax until he got to within 10 feet of the bottom. Steve was just able to reach solid ground as he hung onto the last rung.

Hoping to traverse around the head of the box canyon to where the bighorn was lying, Steve started down a narrow chute about 200 yards long. He left two ropes dangling after he half-rappelled, half-slid down 10- to 12-foot drop-offs. At the bottom, his hopes rose. Off to his right, it appeared possible to walk around the head of the box canyon to a point above the ram. Down another chute he went, descending 100 yards and leaving his last two ropes hanging from another pair of drop-offs. Then he finally spotted the scattered white remains of his sheep. He turned over the largest mass of remains, and there lay the skull, horns intact.

As he began to load the skull into his backpack, one horn slipped off. It stank, but this trophy, which had been a cliffhanger for ten months, was now his. Or it would be—if he got back out. Above him remained a quarter-mile of 45-degree climbing, a scree slope, four roped drop-offs, and 75 feet of swaying ladder. His arms and legs—especially the thighs—were already aching.

The scree was fine, about like coarse gravel. Coming down it was mostly a matter of controlling his slide. Climbing up was awful. With every step his foot would slide almost back to where it had started. He inched his way up, wet and cold from the light rain.

Halfway up the scree, his thighs cramped and locked. He couldn't move them, and he was afraid to move anything else in an effort to relieve the cramps. If he moved, he'd slide. His only hope now seemed to be rescue from above. But to Steve's amazement, after a few quiet minutes, the cramps went away. He was able to go on.

Arriving at the bottom of the ladder was a mixed blessing. Steve was almost home. But he still had that swaying climb. He sent the backpack and other gear up on the safety rope. When the rope returned, he tied it around his waist and started up himself. The higher he climbed, the tighter he tensed, and the more his strength ebbed.

He could hardly move when he reached the place where the ladder dropped over the edge. It was all he could do to hang on. Also, on the way down he hadn't noticed that one of the ladder's sliding oak rungs had hung up on the rock rim. Because it wasn't resting on the knots as it should have, there was a 2-foot gap between rungs. Steve was so weak that he just stood there, unable to raise a leg that high.

Steve hollered to his three friends, who heaved as one on the safety rope and hauled him up those 2 feet and over the edge. The feeling of solid rock under his belly at that moment was something he still can't adequately describe. The long hunt—a once-in-a-lifetime adventure—was finally over. The ram's horns are now kept in a place of honor.

# 19

*Under highly stressful circumstances, many marriages fail. Some 80 to 90 percent of burn victims' spouses leave them, because the horrible pain that fire and subsequent treatment bring can lead to temporary, but difficult to deal with, changes in victims' personalities. Gary and Dorothy Franklin are extreme examples of the survivor resiliency that Dr. Al Siebert describes in our introduction.*

IT WAS THE last day of a long-anticipated moose hunt near Alaska's Talkeetna River, and not a hoof print was to be seen. What could be worse than that? The answer turned out to be, "Don't ask!"

Disappointed off-duty Air National Guardsmen Gary Franklin and Scott Weber glumly went about securing their cabin against intrusions by the claim jumpers that frequented the area. They barricaded the windows with $^3/_4$-inch plywood inside, and slid ¾-inch galvanized pipes into holders to wedge the plywood in place. Gary had more vacation time and would be back for another hunt, so they left behind extra fuel and some of his gear. They loaded rifles, ammunition, and Scott's gear into the small, tandem-seat, single-engine Arctic Tern that Gary had rebuilt himself. Gary maintained an HC-130 Kingbird for the Guard and was training Scott in aircraft maintenance as well.

With Scott behind him in the passenger seat, Gary revved the engine for takeoff on their sandbar landing strip. A storm had whipped through the day before, but the sky was clear and only the winds remained.

Just as the green-and-white Tern lifted off and was about to fly over a tributary that cut through the sandbar, Gary felt what every pilot dreads—a shudder through the fuselage. Wind shear! A blast of tailwind blowing as fast as the Tern's forward speed canceled the air flowing over the airplane's wing. No airflow, no lift. The Tern dropped out of the air like a rock, hit the sandbar, bounced, and didn't quite make it over the tributary's opposite bank. The right landing gear broke off and the belly tank split open, leaving a trail of fuel that instantly ignited.

Gary's Arctic Tern slid 40 feet. The flaming trail blackened the earth, but it didn't catch up with the aircraft until it had turned 180 degrees and come to a stop. At that instant, a fiery explosion engulfed the men and plane so completely that nothing but flame was visible.

Gary pushed open the door and jumped out yelling, "Get out, Scott! Get out!" He rolled on the ground, trying to smother the fire consuming him, but rocks beneath him allowed air to continue nourishing the flames. He ran to the river to douse the fire, then ran back to find Scott on the opposite side of the airplane, just standing there, head down, a flaming torch. The plane's fabric had burned away, allowing Scott to slide out through the framework. The seat belt was on the ground, still buckled. Intense heat had freed Scott by burning the straps off where they were attached to the plane.

The nearest water was a puddle in the sand about a foot deep, 8 feet wide, and half again as long. Scott was in shock and hadn't tried to roll in it. Gary quickly threw him in the shallow water and splashed wildly to douse the flames.

Stunned, in unimaginable pain, and driven away from the plane by cartridges exploding in the fire, Gary and Scott stood talking for a long while, trying to fight off shock and decide what to do. Like it or not, all they could do was return to the cabin, which lay three tributary crossings and 600 yards away. At noon, some 50 minutes after the crash, they struggled up the six steps to the cabin—only to discover that Scott's pants pocket, in which he'd carried the key to the cabin, had burned off. But where had it happened? In the plane? The puddle? While they'd been wading through a tributary? There was no time for Gary to go looking. Scott was shaking violently. He needed to be inside.

Gary remembered that there was an ax under the cabin. With burned chest and arms, he painfully crawled 20 feet over and down across the sand to recover the ax from under a garage-like attachment 4 feet lower than the main building. Crawling back uphill with the ax was an even more painful experience.

The only way in was through a window. The glass broke easily, but Gary's first blow against the ¾-inch plywood took all the skin off the palms of both his hands.

I can't do this! he thought. And then he looked at Scott. Skin doesn't burn. It melts. Scott's features were gone. He looked a bit like a head-shaped candle that had passed through fire.

He knew he had no choice. Gary whaled away at the plywood, ignoring the pain until he had a hole big enough to reach into. He slid out the pipes and pushed the plywood out of the opening.

After removing the glass shards, Gary struggled through the window so he could open the door from the inside and get Scott into a sleeping bag. He wrapped Scott's hands with towels, got a fire started in the pot-bellied stove, and took a long, hard look at their situation. There were no batteries for the two-way radio in the cabin. The airplane's radio was destroyed by the fire, as was the ELT (Emergency Location Transmitter), which upon the impact of a crash sends a signal for rescue teams to zero in on. And the flight plan Gary had filed indicated that Scott and he would return a day later. They wouldn't be missed until tomorrow, and both men feared they might not survive that long.

The only hope for a prompt rescue was in the fact that there was another cabin about five miles down the river. Gary had seen the owner flying around the day before. He was probably still there, and of course he would have a radio in his airplane. Being burned over more than 50 percent of his body made Gary doubt that he could walk that far. On the other hand, though Scott's burns covered only a little bit more skin area than Gary's, he was in far worse condition. Gary had suffered burns mostly on his chest and arms, and a little on his face. Scott's burns were on his face, hands, and legs, and they were considerably deeper. Once again, Gary had to try. He stoked the stove and told Scott his plan.

The parting was sad and mostly silent. Scott's singed throat would not permit a comment, and Gary wouldn't say it, but inside, each man thought he would never see the other alive again. Scott was almost totally dependent on Gary now, and his feeling of helplessness intensified as he listened to his friend going down the steps.

The Talkeetna River winds around in a mile-wide flood basin, but where it passed the cabin it divided into three, and sometimes four, separate channels, each about 6 feet wide. Gary could walk the sandbars and stream edges, and when he needed to cross a channel or tributary, it was only knee deep. But about two miles downriver, the separate channels rejoined into a single channel about 12 feet across and of unknown depth. Gary walked out 5 feet. Swiftly flowing water up to his chest swept him off his feet and down the chute. Swimming was a struggle with his burned chest and arms, but finally he was able to grab hold of a sandbar and pull himself onto the opposite shore, only to find himself trapped in a dead end.

Exhausted, Gary lay resting for half an hour before he could attempt the swim back across the chute. He was less than halfway to the downriver cabin, daylight was already fading, and each crossing would become more and more difficult. The river here no longer snaked back and forth within the mile-wide basin, but flowed from one edge all the way across to the other. Where the channel touched the basin's banks, Gary's way was blocked on both sides by dense brush that it was impossible to fight through with his badly burned body. He would have to go back, his hopes dashed for a rescue on that day.

♦

Back at the cabin, Gary promptly rebuilt the fire and gave Scott a drink. He had read that burn victims need water frequently to avoid dehydration, so Scott was getting it every 15 minutes. About 5 P.M., roughly six hours after the crash, Scott started throwing up black vomit. Common in burn victims, that continued every half hour or so. Taking care of Scott's needs, Gary got very little sleep that night.

Early in the morning, Gary was able to split some firewood from 18-inch log sections with only an ax—no wedge. This was extremely painful given that he had no skin on his palms, and nausea had set in. By noon, he too was vomiting black and could scarcely drag himself off the bunk.

On that morning of September 8, Cindy Brenton, at the Automated Flight Service Station in the Anchorage office of the U.S. Federal Aviation Administration, noticed that the men were overdue according to their flight plan. An Alaska Air National Guard HC-130 was in the air quickly to search for Gary's wrecked Arctic Tern.

About 2 P.M., Gary heard the drone of engines and staggered outside with a mirror in an effort to signal. He was too late. It flew on.

Meanwhile, the Arctic Tern's failure to arrive at Talkeetna according to plan touched off a search by aircraft from the Civil Air Patrol, Kulis Air National Guard Base, and Fort Richardson. A Sikorsky UH-60 Blackhawk helicopter was crewed by Chief Warrant Officer Charlie Hamilton, aircraft commander; Captain Jerry Kidrick, co-pilot; Sergeant Tracy Hartless, crew chief; and para-rescuemen Senior Master Sergeant Bruce Hickson and Master Sergeant Mark Mahoney. The chopper would fly low over the Talkeetna River and coordinate the search with a small Civil Air Patrol aircraft and an HC-130 carrying a training flight crew—all friends of the missing men from Kulis.

♦

At 5:45 p.m., Gary's wife, Dorothy, returned home to find her answering machine maxed out with messages that had started collecting at 10:45 a.m. She learned that her husband's airplane was overdue at Talkeetna. The callers wanted to know where the cabin was located.

Dorothy calmed their five-year-old daughter, Cory, as best she could and called the Rescue Coordination Center to give them the cabin's latitude and longitude. Gary had wisely left a map of where he would be in case of an emergency.

About 7 p.m., Dorothy received an encouraging call from a friend whose ex-husband was on the HC-130 that flew past the cabin. He had called his ex-wife, and she relayed the message that he had been able to identify the airplane, and that it was not wrecked. The hope given by that erroneous message was destroyed when Dorothy called the Rescue Coordination Center to learn the status. "There is a helicopter at the crash site," she was told.

Those last two words crushed her. Before Dorothy and Gary met, she had been engaged to marry an HC-130 pilot who also routinely airlifted supplies to Alaska bush villages in his Piper Super Cub. As he was taking off one day on a 700-foot dirt strip at Ship Creek north of Anchorage with a load of empty nitrogen bottles, a tarp marking the runway blew up over the plane's tail and stuck on. Men on the ground tried to alert him, but he didn't notice and wasn't aware of the tarp. Unable to get enough lift, he crashed into the tops of some trees off the end of the runway and perished in the fire. Dorothy was terrified that the same tragic disaster may have struck her a second time.

She called Command and Control at Kulis Air National Guard Base, but it was too early for there to be reliable information. She was comforted by what Gary's colleagues at the base thought they knew about the situation. "There were two burn victims in the crash, but they are only transporting them to Talkeetna, so we don't think they're badly burned," they told her.

Darkness had closed in at the cabin. Firewood had run out, little water was left, and both men were too sick to do anything about it. Gary's throat had been singed by the fire, and Scott's was worse. Neither could speak above a whisper. They couldn't possibly survive through the night, and if para-rescuemen did arrive, Gary worried that he wouldn't be able to let them know he and Scott were inside.

Around 8:30 P.M., the Blackhawk crew spotted the burned wreckage and landed nearby. Bruce Hickson and Mark Mahoney jumped out and found a burned glove and tracks running two ways. Looking in the direction of the majority of tracks, one of the men saw the darkened cabin.

Gary heard the chopper land and managed to raise himself to a sitting position. Scott could not.

Suddenly, someone was on the deck! They were knocking on the door! But they couldn't hear the "Come in!" the men whispered from inside. There was considerable confusion about whether they had the right cabin, but they knocked again.

Gary and Scott both tried to form the words with their mouths and shout. Grunts and squawks came out.

To the men outside, it proved that someone was in there. But was it an old woman, as one thought, or perhaps an angry loner with a shotgun defending his gold claim? Gary thought he heard one rescuer say, "Let's go. The chopper's low on fuel." He tried to yell, "No! No!" Again, it was mostly a squawk or honk. One man thought that the "No! No!" was "Come in." The other heard it as a snarled, "Go away." They looked at each other, shrugged, and, ready for anything, pushed open the door and saw the burned men.

One man's hand reached out. "Are you Gary?" Bruce Hickson asked. Gary nodded.

Scott, bloated out of recognition and face melted away, never moved.

Mark Mahoney suggested that they'd need two more pairs of hands to carry the victims down the steep, brushy, and muddy incline between the cabin and the helicopter. They told Gary and Scott to hang on; they'd be right back. They returned with Crew Chief Tracy Hartless and co-pilot Jerry Kidrick. Pilot Charlie Hamilton moved the Blackhawk closer to the cabin and shut down the engine to conserve fuel.

On the helicopter, the para-rescuemen could do little to relieve the victims' pain. They tried to put IVs in their arms, but couldn't find veins and didn't want to risk making incisions. They did place oxygen masks over their noses, but that made Gary nauseous, and he vomited every time he had it on. Finally, they put the mask on loose so he could knock it off before his nausea turned into full-blown vomiting.

With the Blackhawk low on fuel, they flew to the town of Talkeetna and transferred Gary and Scott to a Medi-Evac chopper for the flight to Anchorage. Dorothy finally learned the full truth when a neighbor, who that night was also serving as duty officer at Kulis Air Guard, called back to tell her that Gary and Scott were being transported to Providence Hospital. Friends drove Dorothy there and took care of daughter Cory.

When they arrived, Gary seemed stable and alert. He talked about a boat he had wanted for a long time. "Did you hang that 3-D picture?" he asked. "Did you get my watch from my left shirt pocket?" Dorothy dug the shirt out of the garbage and found it, feeling that Gary was going to be fine. But she was uncertain about Scott. His face was black, and he was trembling.

A day later, Gary was so swollen that she could barely recognize him, and even then she couldn't be certain it was him until she looked at his feet.

Nourishment, as soon as possible, is important for burn patients, and so with great difficulty, on September 10, they ran a feeding tube through

Gary's nose to his lower intestines. He already had a breathing tube, and installing another was making him cough and gag and gasp for air.

On the 11th, they removed the breathing tube, and Gary could now communicate without a notepad. He wanted real food and chocolate milk. The next day, he asked for ice cream and more chocolate milk. He talked and joked with his daughters from a previous marriage most of the day. On the 13th, he had his first grafting surgery session, eight hours long. It went well. Gary needed another tube inserted into his stomach to remove the overflow from his feeding tube.

Aside from minor setbacks, the healing process seemed to be going well, even if it didn't sound that way during the daily "tubbings." With over half their bodies burned raw, Gary and Scott were being immersed in bleach baths. Gary's daughters and Dorothy felt it themselves when he moaned, cried out, and almost screamed in extreme pain. On the 15th, he was in such pain that he was getting 15 milligrams of morphine along with 2 milligrams of Valium every 15 minutes. Mostly it didn't help.

At 6:25 A.M. on the 17th, Gary got his tubbing before the 8:30 A.M. operation on his left arm. That went well, but when Dorothy arrived at 7 A.M. on the 18th, Gary looked at her and said, "Get me out of here; they're doing nothing but making me worse." He didn't remember his operations, and he was acting combatively with the nurses. One noticed that his left leg was very swollen when she attempted to change his dressing.

A specialist called in to do an ultrasound found a blood clot that had been caused because the femoral arterial line had been in his leg for too long. They immediately started him on Heparin, a blood thinner. That started a chain reaction that would lead to Gary being called "The deadest man alive." By 4:30 P.M. he was having trouble breathing. His oxygen level was low.

"What do you look for," Dorothy asked, "if a piece of the blood clot broke off and went to his lungs?"

"Shortness of breath," the nurse replied, "and falling blood pressure." She checked his blood pressure, and it was very low—71/50. She administered Dopamine, called in more nurses, and escorted Gary's oldest daughter, Tracy, and Dorothy out of the room.

In minutes, they heard over the loudspeaker: "CODE 99 ROOM 2026. That was Gary's room, and after ten days in the hospital, they understood the code. Gary had stopped breathing. Dorothy sat on the waiting room floor praying.

After medical personnel revived Gary, a line was inserted into his heart to measure the pressure of the blood flow. At first they thought that a piece of blood clot had in fact lodged in his lungs. Then they considered open heart surgery, with a 50/50 chance of survival. Gary was given a paralyzing drug, and his arms were tied down so he couldn't be combative.

More specialists had been called in. The so-called "bug doctor" administered the antibiotics Gary would need if he was hit with a bacterial shower of a sickness called septicemia, which can quickly become systemic. Another reviewed the chest x-rays. And yet another checked Gary's adrenal level, which was very low. He administered a large dose of cortisone.

At 1 A.M., Dorothy was told that nothing more could be done for her husband. His stomach and kidneys had shut down. A ventilator kept him breathing. His blood pressure was falling rapidly. This was now the seventh time Gary's heart was pumping below what is considered as-good-as-dead. That's about 50/60. His was as low as 20/40. The duty doctor signed the medical record indicating that Gary had died and told the nurses that he would catch a little sleep. He asked them to call him when Gary's heart actually stopped beating.

A nurse with the bedside manner of a viper came into the waiting room and told Dorothy and Tracy to go say their good-byes. No man as sick as Gary could be talked or prayed back to health. Only a miracle could save him. She single-handedly crushed any hope Dorothy had left.

Tracy would not say good-bye. She yelled at her dad not to leave her. She reminded him of the good times, like the Brownie Banquet, when he flew in to attend it with her.

Within an hour Gary's blood pressure began to rise. Gary's dad, Don, stayed with him all night, running to the waiting room to call out each new increase in blood pressure. Was it Tracy's coaching? Or the large dose of cortisone? The many prayer groups assembled in the middle of the night? Dorothy was convinced that his recovery was indeed a miracle. She remembered incidents like the one when her brother at home suddenly sat up in his bed, feeling the need to phone her. That had been the exact moment when Gary had been at his worst.

Throughout the night, Dorothy would go in and whisper to Gary, then leave the room again. Sometimes she was too frightened to stay, because she could not bear seeing him die and be helpless to do anything to save him. But at 7 A.M. that Sunday morning, Dorothy felt a peacefulness come over her.

The duty doctor came down about 9 A.M., saw Gary's room empty, and was about to yell at the nurses for not calling him, when he recognized Tracy's voice. She was still talking to her dad. They had moved him to another room.

In a few more days Gary was recovering well. On the 27th Dorothy needed to drive her father to the airport, and she stopped at the hospital first so he could say good-bye to Gary. This was the first time Gary did not wake up to speak to them when they entered his room. Dorothy had a bad feeling about this, and hurried back from the airport to find Gary's heart rate dropping to half of what it had been. She called the nurses; they called the doctor. About that time, their minister, a retired doctor, stopped by to pray with them and asked that Gary have a CAT scan. He believed that Gary was suffering from subdermal hematoma.

Sure enough, the blood thinner had set a blood clot on the brain to bleeding. The left side of his brain was swollen with fluid and blood.

Emergency brain surgery was required, and the doctors told Dorothy that Gary probably wouldn't be able to speak and might become comatose because of that bleeding.

The doctors drilled two holes to drain fluids from the brain and advised Dorothy to get some sleep, because Gary would be heavily sedated for twenty-four hours. She called in to check on Gary's status throughout the night and early morning.

When Dorothy and Tracy walked into his room later that morning, Gary gave them a thumbs-up. The doctor still believed that Gary would have a speaking problem.

"Gary is sounding out words and writing them on a dry-erase board we brought," Dorothy said. "Could that make a difference?"

The doctor smiled. "Gary will be just fine."

To avoid further bleeding, Gary came off the blood thinner, and a drainage bulb was installed to keep as much blood as possible away from the brain. Dorothy elected to have a "bird's nest" put in a main artery between his leg and stomach to catch clots before they got into his lungs or heart. On the 30th, they did an echogram of Gary's heart through his esophagus, to see if it had been affected by the bacterial spray. The echo was normal.

That day, one of the doctors checking drainage told Gary about the surgery on his head. He was angry, and glared at Dorothy, who became so upset she walked out and around the corner. She could hear the nurse explaining all the difficult decisions Dorothy had had to make in these last weeks. Gary had immediate regrets. "Ask her to come back in," he said.

Gary reached out with his arms, and put his right arm around her as best he could and said, "I love you." Dorothy cried as she had so many times since September 8.

A week after being moved to the Primary Care Unit, Gary was asked to submit to one more graft. He was doing fine, but the nurses on the fifth floor, who didn't specialize in burn patients, were unaware that

Gary needed bleach tubbings to kill germs and clean his skin. Dorothy called it to their attention, as did one of the Thermal nurses. But the doctor hadn't ordered it, so it didn't happen, which is an indication of why the medical profession in America has become our fourth most dangerous health threat.

The day after the surgery, Gary's back was a mass of open sores again. He now had to suffer tubbings twice a day. He was released from the hospital a week later, but the tubbings continued up to three times daily. In two weeks his back had healed, but seven months after the accident, his right elbow still had not. It was necessary to peel back a patch of skin from his stomach, leaving one end still attached there, and graft the patch onto the elbow. Gary couldn't move his right arm for thirty days.

Meanwhile, Scott was much worse. His hands were so badly burned that the doctors considered amputation. Then they decided to let the hands stay, for aesthetic reasons only. To get skin to grow back on them, the skin on his stomach was slit open, and his hands were inserted between the stomach's fat and skin layers, then sewn back up. Now that his hands were in that position, skin would grow back on them. But Scott could not move either hand to scratch, blow his nose, feed himself, hold a phone—nothing for thirty days! His legs, which were suspended up in traction, made it all more horribly uncomfortable. Swivels in the traction harness allowed him to move his legs like he was riding a bicycle, but this was his only movement for the entire month.

When his hands were removed, the skin had grown around them like mittens. It had to be cut to separate the fingers. Handprints remained on Scott's stomach.

Scott also had a serious case of septicemia in his skin grafts, but despite being burned deeper and over a little more of his body, he did not "die" of complications seven times as Gary had. On the other hand, Scott was told he would have to find different work. Because of damage to his hands, doctors were convinced he'd never go back to being an airplane mechanic. He did, however, and he still works as one in Australia. His face was rebuilt, but he looks nothing like he once did.

Two months after his last operation, Gary was having problems with his therapy. He needed to stretch his skin to keep it pliable, but it kept splitting, and he couldn't raise his right arm above his shoulder. Surgeons took a muscle from his back and a patch of skin from his upper thigh and inserted them under his armpit to compensate for shrinkage in that area. Again, there was much pain and discomfort, with his right arm tied to the headboard of the bed as he tried to rest on two vacuum containers. One sucked residual blood from the place on his back from where the muscle was taken, and the other from the armpit where it had been inserted.

Gary was becoming very angry with Dorothy after the surgery. She wasn't able to make him comfortable, and at one point he told her to go home and just forget about him. Amazingly, little five-year-old Cory stepped in and actually talked sense into them both.

Since so much attention goes to the extreme measures necessary for physical recovery, Gary found that people in such situations don't think enough about how their emotional behavior changes. He was having trouble back at work. Dorothy kept telling him he had changed. He didn't recognize that it was because he was living through torture, and the change was gradual.

For six months, Dorothy had to help Gary in and out of his clothes, and help him bathe. For Gary, bathing was so excruciating that he had to build up to it mentally, then say, "Now's the time. Do it!" It was like ripping off a Band-Aid, but on the level of the whole body.

The reason for that was that the skin was repairing itself—nerves and blood cells were growing back. Anytime nerve ends are disturbed, the pain is intense. If you're out in severe cold for long enough that the blood flows out of your hands to conserve your body heat (the beginning stage of hypothermia), your hands hurt when the blood returns.

If Gary sat quietly in a chair for 15 minutes, the pain would calm down, but if he just scratched himself it was back. He was taking Percocet, a narcotic pain reliever, at the rate of two every four hours, and it did nothing for him. Usually, if someone takes half of one for extreme stress and severe headaches, he'll be out for the day.

At one point after the pain had lessened, Gary was annoyed that it seemed as if Dorothy had lost interest, and was helping him less and less. They were at the stage of recovery where, she knew, the only way to help him more was to help him less. Full physical and mental recovery meant a return to doing things for himself, as he had before the accident.

Today, Gary says he is very lucky that Dorothy stayed with him. She had been told that 80 to 90 percent of married burn victims get divorced, and it took a strong person to go through the struggle she did. Gary himself has proved to be resilient. He has again become what he was, and maybe he's even stronger for the ordeal. Dorothy says she couldn't have survived the way he did. "He is an amazing man," she said.

Asked if he still hunts, Gary said, "I'll do some fishing this summer, and I've been thinking about bowhunting deer. I did that when I was younger, and I can do it right here close to town. You see, Dorothy worries so much when I'm off at a distance."

# 20

*After a horrible clash with a spinning propeller, Verna Pleasure would not let pain and disability keep her from getting back to the person she had been—a person making a difference with her life. When she found one path blocked, she looked for others until she succeeded.*

VERNA PLEASURE lived in St. Mary's, on the Yukon River in Alaska, and was flying home with Larry Ledlow in his Cessna 207. Ledlow ran an air taxi service, flying a schedule, doing charter flights, and taking people where they couldn't go any other way except by dogsled or snowmachine.

When they landed at the airport, they discovered that a terrible snowstorm had closed the seven-mile road to town. It was a bitter day with a north wind of 40 miles per hour and temperatures of 25 below, and the only shuttle service was a snowmobile. That would be a punishing trip. Snow was still falling and blowing. As a favor, Larry offered an option.

"Verna," he said, "I have a passenger to drop off at Pilot Station just 17 miles from here. On the way back, I could land on the river at St. Mary's and drop you off almost in front of your house."

Verna happily agreed.

Larry noticed nothing unusual as he landed on the river's 3 feet of ice at Pilot Station, or when he dropped off the passenger. But when he revved up the engine for takeoff into the wind, he felt the plane pulling to the right. The right wing was a bit low as well. Stepping out for a look, he found a flat tire on his right main landing wheel. Back in the plane, he radioed his agent in Pilot Station, and his home base, to advise them that he would need a wheel and tire and someone to change it.

By this time, a crowd from Pilot Station was gathering above the 25-foot west bank of the river. A plane simply landing in a village of 400 would attract a crowd, but this plane appeared to have a problem. Larry very much needed to keep his engine running. In these frigid conditions, shutting down for more than a couple minutes would prevent it from restarting. And he couldn't have them milling around the plane while the engine continued to run.

"Verna, I need to tell these people not to come down here and that we have everything under control. You just stay in here where it's warm. I'll be back inside shortly, and then I'll stay with you while we wait for the wheel."

Larry walked out past the left wing tip to call to the people a couple hundred feet away, expecting Verna to do what he asked. He knew her to be a very intelligent and generally affable person. However, he could not know that she had also heard of planes occasionally flipping over in Alaska's wildest winds.

Verna was born into a family of seven children in Philadelphia, but she was raised by an aunt in Florida who saw to it that she grew up learning music and ballet and got an education readying her for college. She was a debutante in Philadelphia. She majored in music and education at Fisk University in Nashville, Tennessee, then did graduate work at Stanford University. She was bright and confident, and she fully trusted her educated insight, even though starting a sex education class for girls proved to be too advanced for the times in the community and the high school where she taught.

By the time Verna was sitting in the Cessna 207 with the flat tire, she worked setting up college programs in widely scattered villages for Kuskokwim Community College. Pilot Station was one of those villages, and she knew people here. The Cessna was listing to starboard, and the wild winds whipping down the Yukon River were creating sporadic wing lift, which jostled the plane and frightened Verna out of her wits. She was certain the plane would flip over, and she didn't plan on being in it when that happened. Verna backed out so she could keep an eye on the plane. She intended to walk across the river to visit with the villagers, and she chose to walk across in front of the plane to get there.

Verna was wearing a goosedown-lined knee-length coat with a warm fur collar. Around her neck was a very long wool scarf, wrapped just once and apparently trailing at least 4 feet. She had her face hunkered into her collar to avoid the bitter wind, and didn't notice how that north wind was kiting her scarf south to flirt with the airplane's fast-spinning propeller.

Suddenly, Verna was yanked into something that hammered a sharp pain into the back of her head. It happened so fast that she had no recollection of how she got there, but her head had been slammed into the plane's nose cone. She tried to get away, and was yanked into the cone a second time. By then, the scarf was becoming shredded. That gave her slack enough to attempt another move and allow her to fall away from the propeller. She was terrified that it would take her head off, and she recalled going down in a graceful ballet move and thinking, "I haven't done that in years."

Larry Ledlow had finished talking to the villagers and was starting to turn back to the plane when he heard a flapping sound. He thought that somebody had thrown garbage, or something else, into the river, and the wind had blown it into his prop. He saw fur and feathers flying and ran to the plane to switch off the engine. Then he saw Verna stretched out directly beneath the propeller and ran to her calling, "Verna, Verna, what happened?"

"Well, I'm all right! I'm all right!"

Looking down at her, he could see her left arm still inside her coat sleeve, completely unattached at the shoulder except for a bit of ragged tissue. She had a cut on her neck and a terrible slash across the breast. He

NEVER GIVE UP

189

could look inside and see her heart beating under a membrane. "No, no, Verna, don't move. You are not all right."

Taking off his coat to cover her, Larry was surprised to see that no blood was flowing from her shoulder, neck or chest. Given the 40-mile-per-hour wind and the temperature of 25 degrees below zero, plus a wind chill in the region of 50 below, her wounds were freeze-dried, instantly cauterized.

Fortunately, the crowd of villagers on the west bank included health aides. They added a tarpaulin to Larry's coat to further break the wind.

With the flat tire, Larry couldn't take off to fly Verna to a hospital, but miraculously, a mail plane from Bethel was circling overhead at that very moment. It landed and discharged some passengers, and the pilot came over to see what was wrong. Larry described Verna's wounds, his tire problem, and that the engine was now probably too cold to start. "Stick around a minute," Larry said. "We really need you to fly her to Bethel."

In a moment, health aides arrived with a stretcher and loaded Verna onto the plane. Verna felt that she was roughly pulled onto the stretcher and thrown onto the plane like a dead body. Most of the villagers thought she was already dead, or would be in minutes. And although Larry thought he was asking the pilot to take Verna to the hospital in Bethel, the pilot thought he was hauling a body to the morgue. Verna could hear what people were saying, but she couldn't move or talk. After 25 minutes on the ice, her body was starting to freeze.

By another miracle of happenstance, Verna's body temperature was not likely to rise enough so that she would start bleeding during the flight to Bethel. The plane's heater had failed. And that strong north tailwind helped again by shortening the normal 90-minute flight to about 40 minutes.

The one remaining obstacle was that she couldn't tell anybody she was still alive. She had to find another way. All she could do was try to will her index finger to push up the tarp. By yet another happenstance, the pilot glanced back just as she got it accomplished. He screamed as best a man can, forgot about the morgue, and hurriedly headed for the hospital.

At Bethel, surgeons spent five hours stabilizing her, after which she flew with four doctors to Anchorage. At Providence Hospital, eight hours after the accident, Dr. David Anderson and a team of specialists operated for another five hours. They couldn't reconnect her arm because the propeller had pulverized her shoulder, but the skin could be used for grafts. While convalescing at Providence, some of the Eskimos she so deeply loved came to visit, wrote letters, and lined the walls of her room with cards. Verna never doubted that she would survive, but what gave her promise of a future was that she had a place to return to, full of friends. She had things to accomplish, responsibilities to carry out, and challenges to meet.

In the meantime, however, Verna would become increasingly frustrated as she spent four months in nursing homes. She was a professional trying to get back to the way she was, and all she got was physical care—not necessarily the emotional support she needed. Nurses and Certified Nurse's Aides are hired on the basis of their credentials; their personalities are not screened to make sure that they're well-suited to giving care to disabled people. Nor do nursing homes train new personnel in the special needs of individual patients. Caregivers do what comes naturally, based on their personalities. The younger ones are often more idealistic and try harder. Older ones have sometimes become unhappy with their situations and just try to get through the day. "I found out they were all pulling for me," she said, "but they didn't know how."

Eager to get back to work, and encouraged by doctors who thought it would take her mind off her injuries, Verna discharged herself. By May she had gone back to work for the community college. It was a premature decision. She was tortured by pain. It hurt so bad to breathe that she would hold her breath as long as she could. Her head hurt so much she couldn't connect names and faces. She didn't want anybody to know for fear that they wouldn't give her another chance. But finally, after four weeks, Verna had to admit that she wasn't physically or emotionally well enough to perform effectively in her job.

Verna returned to Anchorage to deal with pain and infection. "It was the hardest time of all," she said. "I felt like I had failed."

By August, she got a major break. A rehabilitation nurse, Virginia Collins, sent Verna to a rehab center in Houston, Texas. These people did understand what Verna needed. They gave her an artificial arm and restored her sense of humor. Still, she knew that she was not physically or emotionally capable of handling the duties of her teaching profession. She would have to find another way to make a difference.

Verna found it at Access Alaska, a nonprofit agency helping the severely handicapped—paraplegics and quadriplegics, often good-looking young men who had motorcycle, swimming, or car accidents. One nineteen-year-old, a motorcycle case, used his head motion to guide his wheelchair. Several others, who could voluntarily move only their heads, used sticks that they controlled with their mouths to run their computers.

Verna walked in cocky as can be, with the idea that her disability and the way that she was coping with it would make her the perfect person to persuade the patients that life was still good. Audrey Aanes, who ran the agency, was immediately impressed by Verna's enthusiasm and convinced that her disability provided her with a key for motivating the disabled. She hired Verna on the spot.

Whether counseling patients, begging for funds, convincing bureaucrats, or even pushing quadriplegics in wheelchairs around the fairgrounds with her one arm, Verna worked in her own style, which she described as like the rain, gentle but persistent. If one way didn't work, she tried another. Verna never gave up.

Propeller blades are smooth and curved. No hooks or corners exist of the type that can grab a woman's scarf. So what exactly happened on the day Verna was hurt would have remained a mystery but for Calvin Kern, an engineer and pilot whose name is on the moon, because of his work with the Apollo 15 Lunar Rover and the suitcase that safely carried equipment for astronautical experiments. He devised a simple test to determine what had happened to Verna.

Calvin tied one end of a scarf to a horizontal clothesline. His simulated propeller was a 4-foot piece of 2-inch molding. Molding has a narrower (or sharper) edge and a wider, more blunt edge, as does a propeller. Calvin would swing the narrow edge at the scarf, which was held perpendicular to the molding by gravity, just as Verna's scarf was held perpendicular to the propeller by the wind. The action was simply rotated 90 degrees.

When Calvin swung the molding slowly to simulate a leisurely rotating propeller, the scarf would begin to conform to the molding at the point of impact, then slide off as the "rotation" continued. If the molding were swung very fast, the scarf conformed to a much greater degree, and the clothesline connection, which simulated Verna's neck, was yanked very hard.

The difference between the dummy propeller and the real propeller was that the molding was not moving in a full rotation, nor was it traveling as fast. It should be noted that the Cessna 207 has a tricycle landing gear arrangement (two main landing wheels, plus a third at the nose), which positions the propeller at 90 degrees to the earth and to Verna's scarf. The propeller of such a plane, hitting the scarf at a direct 90 degrees, would have greater grabbing power than the propeller of a "tail dragger" plane (which has a third wheel at the tail). Such a plane, when on the ground, is mounted so that the propeller slopes back. That propeller would deliver a more glancing blow. Adding further grabbing power still, Larry Ledlow's Continental 300-horsepower engine had a three-bladed propeller instead of the usual two-bladed one. At idle, it turned at a rate of 800 to 900 revolutions a minute. That means Verna and her scarf were facing a minimum of 40 blades every second. As long as the horizontal pressure on the scarf maintained itself, blade after rotating blade could grab and yank. The spinning propeller might also twist and shorten the scarf, in the manner of wringing out a wet towel. In an instant, Verna's head would hit the cone. Evidently, the scarf severed the second time her head hit that cone. With the horizontal tension gone, centrifugal force would sling the shredded scarf remains off the blades. Larry saw no bits of scarf on them after he shut off the engine.

Whether Verna was knocked down by the blades or they hit her while she was dropping to the ice is unknown. All we know is that she fell directly under the prop. Calvin concluded that she was struck by the blades somewhere in their downward motion. He believed that a blade at the bottom of it's rotation would have thrown her out parallel to the wing.

The National Transportation Safety Board (NTSB) investigated and did not issue Larry a citation or fault him in any way for leaving the engine running with a passenger inside. They called it an unfortunate circumstance, understanding that shutting off the ignition in that extreme wind and cold would have left them stranded with an engine that wouldn't re-start. The plane was parked into the wind with the brakes on and would be jostled, but it would not flip over. An inexperienced person wouldn't know that, however, so the NTSB did not fault Verna for getting out.

INDEX

INDEX

INDEX

Whitehurst, Kirk, 49
Widgeon Bowl, 59
wild boar, 109–14
will to live, 2–4, 5, 10, 139
Wilson, Roy, 109
winds, 48–49, 123, 124
wind shear, 45, 124, 172
Winkler, Susan, 68
Woobert, Jake, 166–69
Wowie Zowie icefall, 115–16

Wrangell Mountains, 23–24
Wyman, Donald, 75–82
Wyoming, 159

Y
yellow blackmouth curs, 110,
    111–14
Yezierski, Phil, 49, 54–56
Ysais, Gregory, 141–51
Yukon River, 187

LARRY MUELLER has written adventure tales and a wide variety of feature stories for *Outdoor Life, Field & Stream, American Hunter,* and *Sports Afield.* He was the *Outdoor Life* Hunting Dogs Editor for over 24 years and has authored a dozen books, four of which are still in print.

MARGUERITE REISS' career began with extensive newspaper work, after which she sought out adventure in Alaska. She wrote feature stories for two Alaska newspapers, roughed it as a librarian for a time in a small, remote village, and went on to write stories of wilderness survival for *Reader's Digest, Outdoor Life,* and *Guideposts.* This is her third book.